How To Use God LIFETIME WARRANTY IN YOUR MARRIAGE

Dr. Amos Adeniyi

authorHOUSE®

AuthorHouse™
1663 Liberty Drive
Bloomington, IN 47403
www.authorhouse.com
Phone: 1-800-839-8640

Published by AuthorHouse 11/05/2014

ISBN: 978-1-4969-3572-4 (sc)
ISBN: 978-1-4969-3571-7 (hc)
ISBN: 978-1-4969-3570-0 (e)

Library of Congress Control Number: 2014915170

Any people depicted in stock imagery provided by Thinkstock are models, and such images are being used for illustrative purposes only. Certain stock imagery © Thinkstock.

This book is printed on acid-free paper.

Because of the dynamic nature of the Internet, any web addresses or links contained in this book may have changed since publication and may no longer be valid. The views expressed in this work are solely those of the author and do not necessarily reflect the views of the publisher, and the publisher hereby disclaims any responsibility for them.

Scripture quotations marked KJV are from the Holy Bible, King James Version (Authorized Version). First published in 1611. Quoted from the KJV Classic Reference Bible, Copyright © 1983 by The Zondervan Corporation.

Scripture quotations marked NIV are taken from the Holy Bible, New International Version®. NIV®. Copyright © 1973, 1978, 1984 by International Bible Society. Used by permission of Zondervan. All rights reserved. [Biblica]

Scripture quotations marked NLT are taken from the Holy Bible, New Living Translation, copyright © 1996, 2004, 2007. Used by permission of Tyndale House Publishers, Inc. Carol Stream, Illinois 60188. All rights reserved.

Dedication

This book is pre-eminently dedicated to the Lord Jesus Christ, the author of marriage, who made everything possible, to my wife, Eunice (Yemi), who plays many roles in my life as well as in our children's lives. She is not only my wife, she is a God sent life partner, a good helper in my church ministry and counseling endeavour. She is my best friend, who I can turn to at any time. She is a good role model to our children and many women as well. Above all, Eunice is a dear daughter of God.

This book is also dedicated to our children, who believe in God's marriage institution and to the congregations I have ministered to in Nigeria and Canada.

Acknowledgement

This book, "How to use God's Lifetime Warranty in Your Marriage," is in form of fiction letters. Some of them were based on my almost 40 years insights on church ministry as well as counseling. All marital couples, both in Nigeria and North-America, I would like to thank you all for trusting me. Your stories and struggles have taught me a lot. Even though I didn't use any couple's particular story, the experiences I gained enabled me to think and put my inspirational thoughts into writing.

I would also like to thank my children, Emmanuel and Kehinde for their computer expertise. My wife, Eunice (Yemi), contributed time and her invaluable perspectives to this book. She also spent many hours editing the book. Dr. Grace Adeniyi Ogunyankin used her God given ability to do the final editing, and a big thank you to the rest of my children (Tolu, Taye, Toni and Paul) who contributed in one way or another to the success of this book.

Somebody once introduced me to a congregation about thirty years ago, he said, "this is Amos, he's practically nothing!" I felt offended when he said that, but later on, I came to realize that the guy was right. I am practically nothing without Jesus Christ and God in my life. I do sincerely appreciate God and give all the glory to him for the inspiration he gave me to write this book.

Table Of Contents

Introduction

The idea to write fictional letters to marital couples on how to use God's lifetime warranty in their marriages came into being in the process of a sermon preparation as a guest pastor for a local church in November 2011. I prayed about which message to deliver for many days. About two days before Sunday, I had a dream that a young lady participated during my sermon. After the service, her family thanked me and said I made her speak in public for the first time and I gave her the encouragement that she needs for the rest of her life. Then I woke up.

On the actual Sunday service, during the sermon, I asked the congregation how many of them had a dog or a cat. A young lady – a 17 year old said she had a cat. I asked if she ever took her cat for a walk, she said, "no." I asked, "why not?" She replied, "Nobody does!" Then I said people take their dogs for walks, but this does not mean that dogs are more important or better than cats. Cats have their own usefulness. God who created us knows that we are not the same and that we cannot function in the same way. One should not be boasting that s/he is better than the other. After the service, the grandfather of the cat owner who spoke during my sermon and her aunt came to me and thanked me for the opportunity given to the young lady to talk for the first time in public, which would enable her to express herself publicly. When I was praying at home after the sermon, I had the feeling that God wanted me to tell people to try out what seems to be unusual for them.

It has been my concern for many years that many couples don't take their wedding vows seriously. It is affecting children a great deal; many children have two or three stepparents. Those children without stepparents seem to be the odd ones among their peers. In Canada, about 50% of first marriages may likely end up in divorce. One may presume that the rate of divorce in second marriages would be lower, but instead it is higher at 72% while, third marriages have the highest divorce rate of 85% (Comparative Annual Divorce Rate in Canada). Similarly, in America, the first marriages divorce rate ranges from 41 – 50%; second marriages divorce rate is between 60-67% and third marriages is between 73-74%. (Information on Divorce Rate and Statistics).

This book is fictional. The stories are not real stories. They are about my past experiences with heterosexual couples in my counseling or pastoral care. I do not have a particular person or couple in mind. No names in the book are real names. If anybody's name or any couples have the same names as used in the book, I would like them to know that I am not telling their particular story or using them as an example. The Holy Spirit inspired the writers of the bible stories/

instructions/messages and the same Holy Spirit is still talking to us today. I believe, I was inspired to write the book. I will encourage anyone or couple whose story or stories are similar to what's in the book not to be too critical, but to take it (the book) as a means through which God is speaking to them to change. No marriage is too bad that God cannot change for better. Don't fold your arms and accept your troubled marriage as a done deal. I will advise the readers to call upon the author of marriage, God, through Jesus Christ, to fix their marriages. He is able.

Since the idea of letter writing is becoming obsolete, one may be wondering why letters to marital couples, and not email, text, or any other modern means of communication. Letter writing is an old form of communication, which is to inform, correct, and educate. In the New Testament, there are many letters written by Paul the apostle, and others to individuals and churches to deal with issues, circumstances, and problems faced by the recipients. We never read about their responses or their initial letters to the Apostles. Similarly, only letters written to the couples are featured in this book.

Most of the Letters in this book are long term correspondence with the imaginary couples. The objectives of the letters are to: 1). Encourage couples not to give up on their dream of having a successful marriage and to continue fighting until the victory is won. 2). Enable the counsellors/pastors to keep their counselees' hope alive as long as they are still interested in counselling. 3). Help families and friends to keep on supporting the couples in crises. Note that some of the letters end with prayer, while some didn't. The idea is we don't have to impose prayer on people. Praying with people is as important as praying for people in absentia. We need permission to pray with people, but we don't need permission to pray for people, while they are not there.

In both my pastoral and counselling ministries, the most prevalent issues are marriage and family matters. This book thus serves as a handbook to help couples in crises or prevent couples from getting into a marital mess. It can be used in marriage enrichment groups or as a counsellor/Pastor's handbook. The group Leaders, Counsellors or Pastors should not use the book as a weapon of judgment against anyone, but as a means of correction and education.

The book is calling people who just want a family and not a marriage. Many couples lose love in their marriages. Love is the greatest gift God gives to people but many people do not accept it. They choose anger instead of peace or love from God. The book is calling the readers who are making wrong decisions for wrong reasons. We should not let bitterness, anger, frustration, alcohol, drugs, etc., ruin our marital relationships. The principles of marital solutions in the book focus on God. May God bless you as you read it. Shalom!

Chapter 1
Mary & John – From Choice to Marital Life

Dear Mary,

How are you making out? It has been a long time since we talked. How are you finding your studies? Senior high must be different from junior? At any rate, I believe you are going to make it. Continue to work hard as you always do.

Last time we talked, you told me that most of your friends are going out with boys, do you have anyone yet? I do not totally reject the idea of boy/girl friends at your age, but maturity is highly necessary, before one gets him/herself involved in a relationship. What do I mean by maturity? I am trying to say one must be ready, age wise, to be able to handle any situation that may arise during dating. "I broke up with him/her" is not uncommon with people of your age. One needs to know how to handle a breakup disappointment. I know many people of your age when their relationship broke up, they cried, which almost led to depression, because they felt rejected and abandoned. So you need to be matured emotionally, physically and spiritually.

You should also know that going out steadily with regard to a relationship is time consuming. You need a man in your life, but your education is supposed to be the #1 priority for you now. Cost of living is constantly increasing. Most of the couples nowadays need two jobs to make ends meet. High school education may not give one a good paying job. What I am trying to say is financial security should be considered before a serious relationship. Anything that will debar you from achieving your goal should be ignored or delayed as of now. You must know some female students who dropped out of school because of early pregnancy. It is true that many students are doing it -- have boy/girl friends in high school, but how many of them are be able to discipline themselves sexually?

Mary, I don't want you to think that I am totally against dating at your age. If you know that you are matured enough emotionally and that education will be so important to you- that you will not be wasting your time on the phone,, texting, email etc. – it's okay. I want the best for you, your family is proud of you, they need you, your community, province and country as well. Be smart in your decision. Don't rush, wait for the right time. God has someone for you. The person God has for you will not pass you by. Do I need to say pray or pray more about your life, education, and ask God to give you a man that is meant for you? Do you mind, if I pray with you? Let's pray.

Lord thank you for Mary. I pray that you will continue to bless her, to help her in her studies so that she will be the woman you want her to be. Help her not to be ashamed to be different. Give her the right man for her life at your time in Jesus name. Amen

God bless you Mary, keep in touch.

Dear Mary,

It was so nice to hear about your accomplishments during your high school graduation. I was told that you graduated with honors and that you got a couple of awards and scholarships. Well done lady. You must be happy. I thank God for you. Mary, I am sorry that I was unable to attend the ceremony. Your parents told me that it was wonderful.

Two years have passed since I wrote you a letter, even though we have spoken on the phone a couple of times. Now you are in university, you must find it different from high school. I believe you will make it. You asked me in your email about how to choose the right partner. The answer to your question is very simple, and at the same time, it is not that easy. You ought to ask God, in prayer, for 'Mr. Right' to marry. Many people have chosen their partners in marriage based on beauty, handsomeness, sexuality, education or a good job. Some chose their partners because of' blind love' - love that doesn't see the bad side of the man/woman.

Let me remind you about what Saint Paul said, he urged us not to be unequally yoked with unbelievers. You need to note that a Christian and non-Christian cannot build a home – marriage - together. You need to limit your choice to believers. God who matched Adam with Eve is still there. He is able to bring the right person to you. God knows that it's not good for a man or woman to be alone. He did not only say it, he put it into action (Gen. 2:17). Do not underestimate the role of prayer with regard to choosing the right man. Abraham sent his servant to go and look for a wife for his son, Isaac. The servant prayed to God to prosper his way by choosing the right woman for Isaac to marry. God did it for him. God who did it for Eliezer, Abraham's servant (Gen. 24: 12-21) is able to do the same for you. He is still in business of answering prayers. He is ever the same (Heb. 13:8). Don't hesitate to talk with your parents and your pastor at home to join you in prayer. With God all things are possible (Luke 1:37).

You may be wondering," how long can I wait for"? God's time is the best for a perfect man. Many people rush into marriage and they quickly rush out of it. Don't be like them, wait on the Lord (ps. 27), and he will make you happy by giving you a suitable man. Again, wait upon God, depend on him for the right person, a man who will love you unconditionally (agape love). God wants you to be happy and wants the best for you. Can I pray with you?

Lord thank you for Mary, she needs you to provide a wonderful, loving husband. Please let that person come into her life. And help Mary to know him and love him. Also, help her in her studies and in her walk with you, in Jesus name. Amen. Keep in touch. God bless you.

Dear Mary,

I was delighted to hear the good news about your man and that you are doing very well in your studies. I always enjoy talking to you on the phone, feel free to call anytime. This letter is to fulfill my promise I made during our last phone conversation.

God is good in giving you John. I was told by your parents that he is a good Christian guy. Congratulations, you both need a good start. I will like to suggest to both of you to be sincere to each other. Don't be in the closet. Don't wear a mask when you are together! What am I trying to say? Try to be Mary and John to be John. Don't hide your feelings - if anything he does irritates you, let him know. You don't need to agree with him all the time because you don't want to hurt him. Don't pretend to be someone else, be Mary all the time. To disagree with each other will allow you to have a good communication and to know each other better, but your disagreement should always end amicably. You disagree to agree is great, that is, you agree. I hope you will both do your best to know each other very well. You need to understand each other well, to communicate loud and clear, don't allow misunderstanding and misinterpretation, don't assume, assumption kills relationships. Ask a question when something is not clear to you. Frustration should not find its way into your relationship. Dating can be a time of joy, happiness, support, sharing, laughter, learning and a host of other good things.

I need to say it again; John is John and you are Mary. Don't try to make John be Mary. Men are different from women, and you are also not from the same family. Both of you have a different upbringing. You don't need to judge each other, but to correct each other in love. You don't need to wait till after your wedding before you tell each other your faults, do so now with a good intention. Dating is supposed to be a time of fun, growing together emotionally and spiritually. It is a time of planning. Try to dream together or share your dreams. Share what kind of family you would like to have. What kind of husband or wife you would like to see in each other.

I will try to write you again, feel free to ask me any question you want. But lest I forget, find time to pray and study the bible together. You can study some families in the bible together, see their weaknesses and strengths. Find yourself good books on marriage. I Have some. Let me know if you want me to pass them to your parents to give to you. Give my best regard to John. I am looking forward to meeting him. Let us give thanks.

Jesus, thank you for answering Mary's prayers. Thank you for John's life. Thank you for the time they have spent together. I pray for them for your blessings. Help them to have unconditional love for each other, as you do for them. Thank you Lord again, in Jesus name. Amen

Dear Mary,

Time goes by fast. You are graduating soon. I heard that you got a good job, and that John is doing well at his work. He likes his job, I was told by your parents. I am so happy for both of you that things are going well.

I understand that you have something special on your finger. You are engaged!! Fantastic and congratulations! Both of you are telling people around you that you intend to marry each other. You know that being engaged means that you need to pay closer attention to each other than before. You need to plan your future together. It is time for you and John to find time out of no time to seek God's face and to study his word together. I am happy that you have been reading good books on marriage. Treasure the compelling information and apply them appropriately.

The ring you are wearing is telling you that you are different from all other ladies who are yet to be engaged. Your commitment to each other needs to be greater than before. Your love for each other ought to be based on nothing else, but genuine love.

I am wondering, how long your engagement will be. I am not trying to rush you to marriage. Perhaps you need to have a time frame. At any rate, you need to be focusing more on important things like a place to live, how you will handle your finances, how many children and when, what kind of wedding you will like to have, where to honeymoon, which church etc.? The more you talk and plan together, the more you will understand each other better. The more you know each other, the easier the marital burden on your marriage. When you say yes to each other, which means; I will marry you, you indicate that you have chosen a partner you will spend the rest of your life with. Marriage is supposed to be "until death do us part." You have chosen the father/ mother of your children; and grand and great grandfather/ mother of your grand and great grandchildren, respectively.

It will be a good idea to stay free from pre-marital sex, since you will be looking forward to the time you will be having guilty free sexual intercourse at any time you want it. I will raise the subject of the role of sex in marriage with you as time goes on. Above all, let love (agape love) be in the center of your relationship. I will not mind you sharing this letter with John. I am looking forward to seeing him again. Maybe we can find time to talk; remember face to face is better than a hundred letters or phone calls or emails. And if it is possible, find time to talk to a marriage counselor or your Pastor. Shall we pray?

Thank you for your wonderment over John and Mary, bless them in all their undertakings, help them to be sincere to each other. Meet their needs. Listen to them when they talk to you. Be faithful to them and let them be faithful to each other and to you. In Jesus name we pray. Amen

Dear Mary,

I missed your telephone call last night, but guess what? I got your invitation card today in the mail. I am excited for you, you must be as well. You are wondering if my wife will be able to come, yes, she will. She sends her congratulatory message to you. How can you prepare for the 'D' day was your question.

As I suggested earlier, both of you should have learned a great deal about each other by now. If not, you still have seven months before the wedding. Don't pretend in any aspect of life, no camouflaging - be open to and sincere with each other. Try to transfer the love and commitment you have for each other now to your marriage. Try to grow in what you have planted. If you cannot do better, don't do less, with regards to all things that you have been doing together. Remember, marriage is supposed to be "for better for worse, till death do us part."

A question that you and John need to ask yourselves is, what do we want, a wedding or a marriage? Many couples focus on their wedding, forgetting that a wedding lasts for one day, marriage is forever. Don't spend all your energy on the wedding, plan for it, but don't overdo it. Focus on your prospective home, your incoming children and your parents on both sides will be more beneficial for both of you than fretting over any aspect of the wedding day. Divorce hurts. Everyone in its web is a captive, a loser, and children suffer the most. In order not to get there, it is important to build your home on a rock. A good foundation is highly essential. Have a good plan, pray and invite Jesus Christ to be the corner stone of your marriage. Jesus was present at the weeding at Cana in Galilee, the couple were not embarrassed when their wine ran out. Jesus supplied more and better wine (John 2:1-11). If Christ can be in your marriage, he will help you out when your love, commitment, trust, etc. are running out. Jesus should be the unseen guest at all times in your home.

By the way, are you planning for a big or small wedding? It will be better to cut your cloth according to your size, that is, don't over spend. You don't need a big bank loan because of your wedding. You told me before that you wanted to buy a house. I will assume that you have a mortgage. Perhaps your cars had not been fully paid for. You don't need another big loan. Money issues can be frustrating in marriage. It can ruin intimacy.

Where are you planning to go for your honeymoon? It is better to let it be a quiet place. You need time to rest, time for transition to married life. I will talk more about this again in my next letter to you. Start to pray not only for a good wedding, but also for God's protection over you, your families and others who will be attending your wedding. Keep yourselves well and fit in Christ Jesus. Let us pray.

Lord Jesus, we thank you again for what you are in our lives. I pray for John and Mary as they are getting ready for their wedding. Please protect them and all their loved ones. Bless them and meet their needs, oh God. We want you to start their home with them. Thank you again. In Jesus name we pray. Amen.

Dear Mary,

How are you making out? Can I call you Mrs. Brown yet? Maybe not yet, the time is fast approaching. Thank you for your kind words in your email and when we were talking on the phone. I am glad you followed what I have been saying to you. How much sessions have you done for pre-marital counseling? Take what the pastor is saying seriously. You don't want to get married twice, I believe! You need to do it well and right.

It is not an overstatement to say the success or failure of a marriage depends on how the foundation is laid. Your wedding day, which is fast approaching, needs great preparation that should start with asking for God's help. If you belong to a prayer group, it will be nice to tell them to be praying for you. If you don't have a prayer group, it will be appropriate to call your good Christian friends to be praying for you. Satan is still at work. The prayer of the faithful ones with you will put the devil to shame not only on your wedding day but on your marriage. Even though your first night of your marriage will be at your honeymoon, don't be too anxious about sexual intercourse that you will enjoy for long. Find time to read (I Cor. 13) and meditate on it well. Pray for each other and tell God to make your home a real Christian home, to bless you Mary, to be a good wife (Prov. 31:10-31). John will be happy to have a 'noble' wife. John needs to pray to God to help him to love you as Christ loves the church. Let me remind you again, your wedding announces to the public that you are both one, no longer two. And what God has joined together, nothing should put asunder (Gen. 2:18-25). Plan how to be one in whatever you do and what you will be doing including your finances.

I will like to warn you not to overwork yourselves before your wedding day. Three months seem to be far away, but guess what? It is fast approaching. Make sure you get things ready a week before your wedding day. I hope your rings will remind you of your commitment to each other; they are symbols of your vows. A ring has no beginning or end; this is a typical love of God (agape) which God wants you to have for each other.

After your wedding day, you will be more accountable to each other. You ought to cherish each other more than before. Do not forget to take your bible with you on your honeymoon. While there, try to read Eph. 5: 22-33; Col. 3:18-21; and Peter 3:1-7. Find time to rest, study your bible, pray and enjoy your bodies.

This is my last letter to you before the wedding; I will see you at your wedding and write you after the honeymoon. Feel free to call anytime. Be blessed in the Lord. He will be the foundation of and provider for your home. Jesus loves you. Continue to love each other as he loves you. Shalom!

Dear John & Mary,

Welcome back from your honeymoon. How did you make out? My wife and I were praying for you. We were so happy to be partakers of your glorious (wedding) day. Everything was so good. The service was great. The pastor did a fantastic job. Reception was wonderful; the food was delicious and palatable, the venue itself was a good choice. The wedding was well planned and well organized. Your parents on both sides must be pleased. My wife and I cannot stop thanking God for you.

As you know, your lifestyle is different now. You have to freely share your bodies. You preserved your bodies for this time. Try to enjoy what God had created. Make your sexual life fun and enjoyable. Many marriages are in trouble today because of lack of good sexual intercourse. God created it and you need to do it with much appreciation of yourselves and God's gift. Do it not to punish one another, but to enjoy it together. I am talking about the state of satisfaction. You should both make sure that you reach orgasm during sexual intercourse. If it is reached at the same time, it is great. Otherwise, if it is not too painful, one should try to make sure that the other reaches it, too.

You may ask: "How many times can we have sex in a week or how often?" I cannot dictate a number to you. You have to talk about it and agree on it. Many couples have a number of times like every other day, or two times in a week. You ought to agree on how and when to have sexual relations every week. If one of you is too tired on the agreed day, you should pay him/her back. Don't allow the devil to come into your marriage because of sexuality. Many non-Christian couples are unfaithful to their marriage because their spouse did not satisfy them sexually. Be careful. If any of you want to have communion with God, perhaps fasting, you should tell your partner to join you or that you will not to be able to meet your partner's sexual need for that particular time or night. Do everything to glorify God, even with regard to sexuality.

Do not join others who are in the opinion that sexual intercourse is dirty or an ungodly thing which Christians should not talk about or waste time about it. Each couple should not deprive their partner food, clothing and of course marital rights (Ex. 21:10b). This is God's command to Israelites. Sex is one of the marital rights which God wants for each couple. Paul the apostle told the Corinthian church that the body of each couple belongs to his /her spouse. (I Cor.7:3-5). You need to join millions of Christian couples who really appreciate God for giving them the opportunity to be partakers of beautiful sexual intercourse created by him. If you want us to talk more about the subject give me a call or email me any questions you have. Enjoy each time you have sex to the fullness. God bless you. Let us pray.

Thank you Lord for creating us and for the gift of sexuality, let Mary and John enjoy themselves each time, oh Lord. Bless their marriage, too, in Jesus name. Amen.

Dear John and Mary,

Let me quickly share with you what my wife and I had to undergo thirty years ago. Adjustments! Marriage adjustments as a husband/wife are necessary in any successful marriage. We all need to adjust anywhere we go; buy a new house, move to a new place – city, state, province neighborhood. Any adjustment may not be easy. Perhaps it is worse in marriage.

Since both of you come from different backgrounds and different church denominations, adjustments are needed. In order to be happy together, you have to talk over what to agree on, what to uphold and how to bring up your own family. The first year of any marriage is always characterized with ups and downs because of the adjustments that ought to be made. You should not be afraid to talk about your differences and how to handle them or adjust to them. Adjustments that you need to make or you are making will indicate a sense of how you're working together or the reality of your commitment; that is, it may put your love to test. Time of adjustment is not a time to condemn each other. It is not a time to point an accusing finger at each other. It is not a time to judge or to put down one's family upbringing. You need to encourage each other and be each other's keeper. Be an encourager not a discourager. You need to study the word of God together and make it a standard. Humble yourselves, no pride, I am well trained, my parents are super parents; be careful of such sayings. Don't forget you are now one flesh, no longer two.

Don't look for each other's fault. It may be destructive in any relationship, especially, in marriage. Try to pray for each other. Recognize your wife/husband's weakness and take it to God on his/her behalf. If one of you is a good housekeeper including cooking, the other one should humble him/herself to learn how to do it. If you cooperate with each other, peace will be the product. If A has a bad habit, B should try to bring her/him on the right track. Do not look down on each other, but uplift each other. Try to love and care for the man/woman you marry. Do whatever is in your power to make your partner fit in and acceptable to people in your community. I believe you are meant for each other. God joined you together in marriage for a special reason. Do not criticize or blame God for your choice to marry your wife/husband. Allow adjustment to take place, when and where necessary. If the adjustment is slow, don't worry about it, slowly but surely it will come. Be patient with yourself and with each other.

Let us pray. Christ Jesus, we know adjustments are not easy, but with your help all things are possible. Lord, please help John and Mary with the adjustments that they may likely need to make in their marital life. We trust that you will help and uphold them, in Jesus name. Amen

Dear John and Mary,

I wrote you a few months ago about the necessity for adjustments in early marital life. I am glad you admit that it is so, and I am happy that you are doing your best to adjust to a new life. I want to talk again about a similar subject, change.

As you know, change is one of the things that many people don't like to undergo. Change is necessary and sometimes it is required in our day to day life. Husband and wife must be open to changes in their marital life. They should not be ashamed to ask each other for a change, when necessary. You need to welcome any change that will promote a better relationship between each other. You should not act like many non-Christian couples who may prefer a divorce to a change in their marital lives. I am talking about positive changes in life, since you are from different academic and social backgrounds. You need to beware of superiority/ inferiority complex in your day to day relationship. This may be a stumbling block to a positive change.

As a Christian couple, you need to pray for humility before asking for a change from your partner. You ought to pray for the person concerned to see a change as a form of adjustment. I suggest that you accept any change that will bring glory to God, and more love and understanding into your marriage with thanksgiving. Genuine love, persistence and patience are highly essential when you are working on each other in regards to a change in your marital life.

Why a change? Before you ask for a change from each other, a Godly and meaningful discussion about the subject is necessary. Do not allow an argument, but a friendly discussion to take place. End the request for a change discussion with prayer for God's grace for the concerned partner. Do not allow the devil to bring dispute that can ruin your marriage. In any healthy relationship, changes may be required or needed. We see changes in businesses, in governments as well as in churches. When a change is needed from any of you, the other spouse should be praying until it happens. Perhaps you think your partner needs a change, maybe it is you that needs a change. Both of you have to put yourselves in each other's shoes. God wants you to grow in your relationship, try to grow up together in love. It takes time to see changes occur. Don't be hopeless, be hopeful, up-hold each other in prayer and love. Shall we pray?

Oh Lord, would you please help John and Mary to love each other unconditionally so that they will be open to change when they ask each other. Give them humility, patience, love and grace as they may need changes for the betterment of their marriage, in Jesus name. Amen.

Dear John & Mary,

How is life with you? I am so happy that things are going well with you. In your email you are wondering how to advise your friends, a couple, who tried to separate their beds.

In fact, I wanted to talk about it with you, too. You see, a husband and wife are supposed to be one. They need to share their bodies, share their bed. At the same time, you may need to ask your friends why they are sleeping in different rooms. I know some couple like that, too. One particular wife told me that her husband moved into another room because he would not go to bed with her, he stays up watching television or sits in front of computer. He goes to bed between 2 and 3 am. When he gets to bed the wife would be disturbed. Another husband would not come home from his buddy's house until past 2am, almost every night. Ask your friends and hear what their reasons are.

When one is joined together in marriage, bad nature or bad friends should not share his or her spouse with him or her. Sleeping late or sleeping in a different room may not promote good sexual intercourse. And if that continues the other spouse may find his/her self-satisfaction somewhere else. It is a very dangerous situation. Please for God's sake, go to bed together and share your bodies together. Admire every part of your bodies and use your hand to touch God's creation – that is, the parts of your bodies. Be romantic, it is necessary as sex itself. Be in love all the time; give your bodies for a touch. Touch, embrace and enjoy each other's body – hands, legs, neck and head and also, appreciate the beauty/handsomeness of each other. Word like, "you are so beautiful or handsome" or "I can see the handiwork of God in you" are uplifting. Such words in bed or anytime would make you look forward to be in bed together to see each other after work. You should feel attracted to each other all the time.

I will like to advise you- you can share it with your friends, too- to be reading the Songs of Songs in the Bible. It has only 8 chapters. Perhaps the author is indirectly trying to appreciate God himself or the writer is demonstrating God's beauty in his spouse. You can adapt or adopt this idea of the writer. Tell each other how much you love him/her verbally or in written form. Text and/or send a quick email to say, "I love you." Carry the attitude of love and appreciation to bed each night. Advise your friend to come together again and sleep in the same bed, share with them what I have shared with you. Remember, sexual satisfaction plays a big role in any successful marriage. Take good care of your sexuality wisely. It will be a good idea to pray before and after you have sexual intercourse; prayer of thanksgiving to God, and say thank you to each other. God loves you, he cares for you. Try to love and care for your marriage, and have fun with your sexual intercourse. I will write you again soon. May God bless you and keep you safe.

Dear John & Mary,

It was great to hear from you and to hear that you are doing well. You seem to be happy as a couple and I'm happy that your honeymoon is continuing. That is how it ought to be. Continue being in love.

I am wondering if I have spoken to you before regarding in-laws. I thank God for you that your parents on both sides are good Christian couples. John, I met your parents at the airport a couple of weeks ago. They were so thankful for your wedding and your good beginning. Good news. Keep it up! At the same time, I still feel like talking briefly to you about the dangers in marriage in regards to the in-laws. I hope that you will not allow the devil in your marriage, as it has been happening among many couples. You both need to see or accept that you have four parents now. Mr. and Mrs. Brown are not just John's parents they are yours, too, Mary. Mr. and Mrs. Rice are your parents, too, John. If you can see your in-laws as your parents, life will be easier.

Whenever any of your parents visit you, treat them as you will treat your own parents or as you will like your own parents to be treated. If finances are needed by either side, you are supposed to talk about it before giving money - more so, if it is a lot of money-whether or not you have a joint account. I will be discussing money issues with you later. No negative report about each other to any of the parents. Be careful of the news you share with your own parents without telling your partner. Do not listen to, "why did you allow him/her to treat you like that?" or, "I have never said that to your mommy/daddy". Remember your mom is your dad's wife, not your husband's wife. Above all, see them as your Godly parent. Don't forget to ask them for prayers and Godly advice together. Whatever you do, do it for the glory of God.

Keep the secret within your own home. Be careful of so called friends. Don't say negative things about each other to your own friend or friends. You may likely hear them say: "I will never allow my husband/wife to do or say that to me". Don't be stupid, you have brain, too, you have income, too, and why did you let him/her boss you." These and other comments may likely come from jealous or negative friends. Do not sell out each other to your friends. Keep your challenges between you and God. But if there is any issue that you sense can cause a problem, talk to your pastor or find a counselor. Don't wait for too long before you address a problem. Do not leave fire on your roof while going to bed. Talk over any issue as it occurs. Above all make Christ the unseen guest in your home, talk to him, allow him to advise you and listen to his advice. Let me pray with you.

Father God, thank you for being a good friend and an unseen guest in John & Mary's home. Continue Lord to make them good to each other and let Jesus be their wonderful counselor. In his name we pray. Amen.

Dear John & Mary,

I understand that you are getting busier and busier. Well, it is good to be busy, but don't be too busy. I am wondering if you have good quality time for each other. Remember, you will be busier when you start to raise children, especially if you are both going to keep your jobs.

How are you making out with regard to your time with God? It will be great if you can start your day together with God, that is, if you can read your bible and pray together. When you start each day with God, your lives will be full of energy and hope. Some kind of strength will be there, that is, you will have a sense of courage that you are not alone. God in Jesus Christ is with you." He gives strength to the weary and increases the power of the weak - - but those who hope in the Lord will renew their strength. They will soar on wings like eagles; they will run and not grow weary, they will walk and not faint "(Isaiah 40:29-31) (NIV).

Pray together and for each other. A prayer-less Christian is a powerless Christian. Power, which power are we talking about? Spiritual power and physical power, too. Also, a couple that prays together stays together. When you start your day together in the presence of Christ, you will not end your day fighting with each other, if there is any issue, Christ will help you to resolve it. Try each day to get your renewed energy from Christ. He is always willing to bless those who look unto him for any kind of help.

It will be nice if you can find a daily bible reading devotional booklet which will encourage you to read your bible on a daily basis. The more you read your bible and pray together, the more you will understand your purpose, yourselves and the necessity of loving and caring for each other. Do not worry about anything, but take everything to God in prayer. God cares for you and he wants you to cast your anxieties upon him (I Pet. 5:7 – Ps. 55:22).

Do not hesitate to join a bible study or prayer group in your church, if there is any. The more we grow in the knowledge of the Lord, the more possibility for our growth in the Lord and, the more we grow in the Lord, the more our marital relationship thrives. If you know any Christian couple who fight all the time, check their prayer time or their dwelling in the word of the Lord. I am happy that you go to the same church. Many couples go to different churches, it is not that good. Our number one enemy is always ready, not tired or too busy to fight or wage wars against Christians. The prevailing weapons we have are prayer and the word of God (Eph. 6:10-20). Mary and John, it's so nice to be part of your life. Be blessed in the Lord. Let us pray.

Renew our strength oh Lord. Listen to us when we pray to you. Please continue to encourage John and Mary to be talking to you in prayer and be hearing from you through the reading of your word, in Jesus name. Amen

Dear John and Mary

John wanted me to talk about money with the two of you. In fact, money is one of the greatest enemies of marriage. It may sound funny. Without it, any marriage may likely be in trouble. Too much of it and love of it may be dangerous. Many couples are both working outside home because of financial obligations. In this day, many couples think that they need to make money to make ends meet. In fact, many families do. Everything seems to be more expensive than ten to twenty years ago. It is okay for both of you to continue working outside the home, even when you start raising children. You have to plan it well, find time for each other and the children. You should not let money take the place of each other in your marriage. You need money, but you need each other more than money. Money can buy a lot; but it's not a solution to every need. Money cannot buy a good marriage, where genuine love reigns supremely. Money can buy happiness, but not joy. The love of God in each of you will bring joy into your marriage. Do what you can do to have enough money, but do not let it rob you of your joy.

By the way, how are you managing your finances? What do I mean? Some couples combine their income and each spouse sometimes has a separate spending amount per month. Some couples also have separate accounts but have a certain percentage of their income in a joint account. Some, however, divide the expenses of the household according to the size of the income of both. Which method is best? To me, it doesn't matter. The most important thing is love, understanding and an open mind. Honesty is very important. Be open and honest with each other. Agree on how much to spend, what to buy, and which charitable organizations to support. No big spending without agreement. If there is a need to spend money on your parents or siblings, make sure you talk about it first. Money can be a blessing or a curse in any marriage. We need it to run our marriages. May God help you and guide you on how to be good stewards of money in your marriage.

Shall we pray? Lord, please bless John and Mary more and more. Meet their needs accordingly to your riches in glory. Help them to be good stewards of all the blessings they receive from you. Thank you for their home and jobs in Jesus name. Amen.

Dear John & Mary,

I am glad to hear that in seven months you will be parents!! Wow! Congratulations. John, I hope you are taking care of your child's mom. And Mary, you need to take it easy when necessary. My wife and I promise you our prayers for a safe delivery. If I can share some of my experiences with you – the first child is trial and error. Twenty-nine years ago, when we had ours, it was a big joy and at the same time, a big challenge. Plan for the arrival of the baby, pray for a save delivery and the ability to be good parents.

It may sound funny to know that if care is not taken, your love may be divided. When new parents talk to friends, co-workers etc. about each other- "my wife", "my husband"- may be shifted to "my son/daughter." Be sure not to be jealous of your child. At the same time, both of you should not let your child take the place of your lover. Be reminded, you did not marry because of your future child or children, but because you love each other. The primary goal of God in creating marriage is relationship; to have someone to be with, to talk with, to do things together, to hold and to love. The gift of children is an additional blessing or purpose. Give your child/children the best love you can. You are God's representatives in his/her life/their lives.

My wife and I may likely fly over to come and rejoice with you, when the baby arrives. But let me tell you, in case we are unable to come or come on time, don't be thinking the baby is too little to know what is going on with you or in your home. Be good role models to him/her or them. Whoever you are- loving, caring, supporting, etc. - will be told to the community through your child/children. Plan what kind of training you will be given to your child/children. The book of proverbs in the bible says: "Train a child in the way he (she) should go, and when he/she is old he/she will not turn from it" (Prov.22:6) (NIV). Deuteronomy 6:4-9 says: "Hear, O Israel: The Lord our God the Lord is one. Love the Lord your God with all your heart and with all your soul and with all your strength. These commandments that I give you today are to be upon your hearts. Impress them on your children. Talk about them when you sit at home and when you walk along the road, when you lie down and when you get up. Tie them as symbols on your hands and bind them on your forehead. Write them on the doorframes of your houses and of your gates" (NIV). Perhaps God is saying to you, John and Mary; train your children in the way they should go. You need God's grace and wisdom. It is yours, upon request from God. James 1:5 says: "If any of you lacks wisdom, he should ask God, who gives generously to all without finding fault, and it will be given to him" (NIV). May this be so unto you both, in Jesus name. Amen.

Dear John and Mary,

Congratulations on the safe arrival of your son, Frank. My wife and I are so happy for you. You must have planned for his birth to be close to your third anniversary. Your parents on both sides must be happy. We are rejoicing with them and you, too.

I should talk to you about one of the woes in marriage today- communication. Because of lack of effective communication, many couples had seen the death of their marriages. This is one of the foremost enemies of marriage in our time. You should deal with it carefully in your marriage. Since you have other things to pay attention to, you need to find time out of no time not just to communicate, but to also do it effectively – loud and clear. There are different kinds of communication- verbal and nonverbal communication. If both or one of them is not used wisely, the marriage may be in trouble. You need to talk with each other in the best way to understand yourselves. Do not wear or use masks when you are communicating with each other. If you don't understand yourselves when you are talking, you are only talking, not communicating. You need to listen carefully (most especially when Frank is crying or laughing) to each other and you should not be ashamed to say: "Pardon me," or "what did you say? Or "I don't understand what you mean." Don't forget you are husband and wife, not a prospective couple. You don't need to be afraid of offending when he/she wants you to repeat yourself. It is better that way than to assume what he/she said. Assumption can easily kill communication. Many couples stop communicating because they cannot understand one another.

Don't stop sharing your feelings. Many couples had done so because of poor communication. During dating, the intended couples used to spend hours talking on the phone or when they see each other, what happens after their wedding? The level of their communication starts to diminish until it's too late to adjust it. Continuity of communication similar to dating is highly essential after "I do." Even much effective communication is more needed because couples have more to talk about. Lack of effective communication can reduce the couple's love as well as a good relationship.

I am not saying your communication is not good, but what I am trying to pass across is that if it is good, you need to make it better. If it is not good, you can take what I am saying seriously. Listening is very important, you need to discipline yourselves when you are communicating and also be patient with each other as well as with Frank. Make sure you pass across your message very well and be sure she/he understands or gets what you are saying. We need to be like Jesus. He communicated loud and clear with his disciples and his listeners.

Let us pray. Lord, help us and others. Help John and Mary to be good to each other with regard to communication, let them be patient with each other and Frank, in Jesus name we pray. Amen.

Dear John & Mary,

Frank is one year old already- Happy birthday to him! What a joy to be a mom.
John must be blessed to be a father, and Frank will soon be old enough to
go fishing with him. It is a big job to be parents nowadays. It takes a lot of
commitment to be a wife/husband and at the same time, balance work and
parenting.

I want to talk to you today about commitment in marriage in particular. Many
couples, today, prefer common-law status to marriage. I asked some common-
law couples why they did not get married. They often say that it's because of
commitment. Commitment requires dedication, promise, friendship, obligation,
honesty, faithfulness, trust and so on. Many marriages end in divorce because
one partner or another could not carry on with the vow they made. It is a big
responsibility – a big commitment. Before any couple rushes into marriage, they
have to consider the commitment cost. The commitment we have to friends, at
the workplace, to our neighbors, or in business is somehow different from marital
commitment, it is supposed to be a lifetime contract in a Christian marriage,
marked by agape- unconditional love. We need to do for each other what may not
be easy for non-Christians. The commitment we are talking about is not just give
and take. It is giving and giving until death comes. We need to let go of our self-
centeredness, care more for our partners than ourselves. It is always rewarding.

The good news is Christian couples like you made their commitments before God
during their wedding. When they said, "for better or worse, to love and to cherish"
as long as both of them shall live, surely it was a big commitment, but God being
on their side, they can make it. John and Mary, you are doing a good job. Four
years in marital journey together is not a joke. You don't need to worry about
the rest of the years ahead of you. The Lord who has been helping you is still in
business. Continue to trust him and commit the journey into his sustaining hands.
He will not leave you or forsake you (Heb. 13:5).

It is easy for non-Christian couples to forget their marital vows or commitment,
but Christian couples should try to uphold their unconditional commitment. John,
you need to commit yourself to Mary, and Mary, do the same. Do not allow the
devil to discourage you and reduce your commitment. Many couple did, and the
end was not good. Be faithful to each other. Continue to honor your commitment.
God will continue to do his part in your marital life. Remember, God's lifetime
warranty for your marriage is a done deal, because with him all things possible
(Luke 1:37). I trust that you will be doing your part individually to glorify God
through your marriage. Let your children see how much you commit yourselves to
each other. God bless you richly.

Dear John and Mary,

Congratulations, John, on your recent promotion that would suggest that you are working hard. Mary, you were transferred to another department, good that you are finding the atmosphere friendly than the previous. That is good to know. Caring for one another at home and at work is one of the necessities of human life. Love and care are not only needed at home but they are also needed at work and anywhere. Continue to demonstrate God's love and care at your workplace, the same for John, too.

Since I have been talking about love, let me quickly talk more about it, regarding marriage. People are of the opinion that love is reciprocal. The husband would like to receive back love from the wife, when he gives it. Guess what? Christian marital love is not like that – even though it is good for one to receive love back, we need to show maturity in Christian marital love. Christian love in marriage is not 50/50. It is supposed to be 100%. Each couple would be blessed to have 200% of love in their marriage.

During premarital counseling, I tell many couples to do each other a favor- that is, John do yourself a favor, love Mary. Mary, do vice versa, love John. In most cases, each person always loves himself or herself. No one would hate him/herself and beat or harm him/herself. Each person likes to care for, love and treat him/herself well. Paul says: ".... He who loves his wife loves himself. After all, no one ever hated his own body, but he feeds and cares for it, just as Christ does the church-"(Eph. 5:28-29) (NIV). When God joins a Christian couple together in marriage, they are one, no longer two. One body! That means whatever John does for Mary; he does it for himself directly or indirectly, the same for Mary. You are not John and Mary, but John/Mary. A genuine Christian love in marital life needs to produce happier, healthier, supportive, compassionate, caring, commitment etc. in husband and wife as well as their home. There is no fear in love, perfect love drives away fear, worry, anxiety and tension (I John 4:18).

As I advised you during your honeymoon to read (I Cor. 13), let me elaborate on it. It is a test of love. When you read verses 4-8 exchange love for your name. What love is: John/Mary is patient, is kind, rejoices with the truth, protects, trusts, hopes, perseveres, it never fails. What love is not: John/Mary does not envy, boast; not proud, rude, self-seeking, keeps no record of wrongs, and does not delight in evil. Read these verses as many times as you can. Don't judge each other, but let the chapter guide you. Advise your friends on the chapter. Let Christ be the foundation of your love for each other. The love we are saying here is unconditional love. This is the kind of love Christ has toward us. Christ died for us. He laid down his life because he loves us. Since Christ loves us so much, we ought to love one another. A Christian couple, like you, needs to love and care for each other. I hope you will also continue to have sexual love (eros type of love). Let us pray.

Thank you Lord for your love for us, help us to love one another unconditionally. Please continue to bless John and Mary, let your love continue to bind them together and transmit this love to Frank and others. Amen

Dear John and Mary,

You have been blessed with Rose, wow! She is a big girl, 9lbs! Congratulations. My wife says the same. How is Frank reacting to his sister? They will be playing together in your big yard soon. Your driveway is also long enough for them to run up and down. You are blessed with a safe and quiet neighborhood. Mary is off from work for one year. It is a good idea again. Mary, find time to rest and care for your family and yourself. With the addition of Rose, you must be busier! Enjoy your time off work, God bless you and give you enough energy and wisdom of good parenthood.

Allow me to talk to you this time on another killer of marriage – bitterness. It is a big killer of any relationship. Many marriages, today, end up in separation or divorce because of lack of forgiveness. By the way, forgiveness, reconciliation and restoration go hand in hand, especially in Christian marriages. God forgave us, reconciled us with himself and also restored us to our former position through Jesus Christ. This is what Christian couples ought to adapt in their marital life. It is lacking in many homes today, in non - Christian homes in particular.

Mary and John you are an "image" of God, you should learn how to forgive each other in your marital life. You might have heard people say I can forgive, but I can't forget. God forgave us and he forgot that we offended him before. Is it easy to do? I don't think so. This is the reason why we all need him and his Grace to be like him. Matt. 5:48 say: "be perfect, therefore, as your heavenly Father is perfect." God loves all people. "He causes the sun to rise on the evil and the good, and sends rain on the righteous and the unrighteous" (Matt. 5:45, read it from 43-48) (NIV). If the act of forgiveness is not practiced, couples may likely end up in a fight most of the time, when they remember yesterday's matters or offences that were not yet settled or forgiven. I love the story of the lost son in Luke 15:11-32. A forgiving attitude will break the cycle of any malice.

Do not leave fire on your roof before you sleep! Issues that are not settled before you go to bed are more harmful than a fire on the roof. Do not give the devil a chance. Each one of you should not be too proud to say, "I am sorry" to each other. When I am sorry is said by A, B should be like God and forgives A. You also need to let go. People will say: "let go, let God." Forgive all the time without any reference to the past, that is, what you did last week, last month. Past is gone, and let it go forever. Jesus wants us to forgive one another 70x7= 490 times in a day (Matt. 18:22).

When forgiveness takes place, reconciliation needs to follow in any good relationship. God wants us to be at peace with each other. Restoration must follow reconciliation. After forgiveness, reconcile, and restore each other – peace will reign again in a marital relationship. Friends, don't forget that couples who don't forgive one another may have a broken marriage and even a broken home. Be careful. May God in Christ continue to give you the ability to let go and let him have his way in your marital life. Amen.

Dear Mary and John,

Nice talking to you on the phone last week. How are things with you? I hope that you are having fun with each other. I discussed with you about change in marital life and the importance of making changes if we want our marriage to be healthy.

A key change you need to consider is letting go of old friends. What do I mean? You should know that you are no longer two, you are one. John, any of your old friends who don't want to be Mary's friend ought not to be your friend. This goes for Mary, too. If there was any old girl or boy friend you have to say bye to, bid them farewell for good. No texting, emails, phone calls, and etc. In order to be in a good relationship with your husband/wife, avoid that kind of friendship. It is very risky and dangerous. Any of your old friends, regardless of the gender should know their boundary now. They cannot just call on you without involving your wife/husband. Your single friends can still be your friends as long as they are ready to come to your house or you go to theirs together. I understand that there could be occasions when you want to be with friends separately, just be careful. Always remember that you are one. Spending a lot of time with your single friends as you used to do may cause problem in your marriage. I am not saying you should abandon your old friends totally, but let them know that your life has been changed and that you should be doing things with your spouse. You don't want to continue being single that was one of the reasons you got married. When you go out with only single people, they may likely want you to stay out late or dress like them and so on. It doesn't work that way. What God has joined together, no old friend should put asunder.

What about your old friends who are married? Yes, they can still be your friends. Any of them maybe welcome, as long as you are in the same boat- that is, you have the same ideology. Any friend who holds the opinion that it is possible to have a good marriage, even when there are some marital problems, can be in your lists of friends. I am sure, down the road, you will be meeting friendly couples with whom you will be doing things together, such group like that can be found at church, at work, or in your neighborhood. Be selective - let the Holy Spirit lead you as you choose your friends. Do not forget that the best friend you need all the time is Jesus Christ. He will not mislead or betray you or forsake you whatever happens.

Dear John and Mary,

It is nice to know that you like Toronto, it must be different for you. Well, we all need adjustment whenever there is a change in our lives. I hope the children will grow to like the big city!

Time flies so fast! Your 10th anniversary is coming up. Are you planning for a big celebration? You deserve it. As you know, many marriages end up in separation or divorce before their 10th anniversary. You are one of the less than 50% who survive the first tough ten years of marriage. If you are not planning for a big party, it will be good to have a getaway weekend. I hope either set of your parents will be coming to celebrate with you and be able to babysit for you, if you are to get away. And guess what? It would be wonderful, if you could invite young couples in your church and your neighborhood to celebrate it with you. You don't need to have a big party, maybe just finger food. This will give you an opportunity to share your marital journey and that may give couples who are struggling courage to face their marital challenges. Pray about it, and decide. You will probably be able to bless others or God can save other marriages through you. In fact, you can think of leading a group, maybe in your church or home – if in your church, you will need to talk with your pastor – the group can be a marriage support group. You have enough experience, 10 years to help others, young couples in particular. Many couples' marriages are hurting today because there is not a role model or a support system to talk to about their struggles. This will not only help them know that they are not alone, it will also enable them to learn from their leaders. Marriages in the bible may be part of where discussions can be focused. You can also pick good books on marriage that deals with different topics like; love, commitment, communication, forgiveness, trust, finances, parenting, etc. If you need any help with regards to finding good books, let me know and I will try to help out.

The good news is, the more you try to help young couples, the better your own marital life will get. When you listen to others' mistakes, you will try not to fall into the same traps. If you know good Christian marriage counselors or pastors who believe in "marriage forever," you may invite them occasionally to give talk. All of you will be blessed through their wisdom. In fact, I will be delighted to come over sometime, maybe to your 20th or 25th anniversary. Why not? Do not worry about how to start or lead the group. Since it is going to be based on God's principles, He will be teaching you what to do or say.

How are your children making out? Say hi to them for me. Let us pray. Thank you Lord for John, Mary, Frank and Rose, we pray for more of you in their lives. Keep them safe in Toronto, thank you for John and Mary's upcoming anniversary, help them and teach them how to help other couples. Be all in all for them. In Jesus name we pray. Amen.

Chapter 2
Brad & Amy – Don't Forget Your First Love

Dear Brad and Amy,

How are things with you? It was nice to meet you at the airport last week. How are you making out these days? I am happy that you trust me to share your marital struggles with me. As I suggested to you, communication is one of the issues you need to deal with. Is there any improvement yet? It takes time but it is very necessary.

Most of the time, we always think we are communicating with our spouses, but instead we are just talking. Talking is when we are speaking with the assumption that the person we are talking with understands or should understand what we are saying. We talk, we don't listen or pay attention to the person we are talking with. We talk without passing the information across. Lack of effective communication does not only kill marriages, it buries it, too.

When you are talking with each other, it will be better to clarify what you are saying to each other, you can ask questions about what you just said to let you know that he/she got the message. The other partner needs to ask questions, too, to make sure that you understand or got what he/she was saying. For instance, if Brad says: "I will be coming home late tomorrow." That is communication but not effective. Brad just spoke, he didn't communicate with his wife, Amy. Brad needs to say: "I will be late from work tomorrow, we have an executive meeting at 4 pm, and the meeting will be more than one hour." If you (Amy) are wondering when you should be expecting Brad with regard to the previous sentence- I will be late from work tomorrow – you can ask why will you be late? Or do you have to work late, if so when can I expect you home? Amy, you should not assume that Brad will be late just for 30 minutes or so; ask him, instead of getting worried and wondering what Brad is doing and when he would be at home.

Reflect on how you have been communicating with each other. Try to correct yourselves, Make up your mind individually to communicate with clarity. Ask questions, instead of making assumptions that he/she is saying this or that. When you are talking about an important issue, you don't need the T.V. or Radio on. Listen to each other carefully watch each other's body language, too. Find time to talk about matters that are important in your home. If you cannot conclude or reach decision on the particular issue, you may defer it till next time, except if it is a fight. You need to settle the matter or resolve the fight before you go to bed. Don't pile up unsolved issues. In a good marital communication, there is no Mr. or Mrs. Winner or loser. Let the devil be the loser when you are communicating. Do not agree to disagree; spend good time to talk about important matters. It is better to spend time ironing things out now than have problems later. Some couple may say they don't have time to have effective communication, but later on, they will end up spending hours with their lawyers, when separation or divorce procedures are going on. Spend time now to save time later. Let me know how you are doing. Please get in touch. God bless.

Dear Brad and Amy

It was my pleasure sharing my opinion with you. Thanks for your nice comment. I hope you will keep on having effective communication. You wanted me to write you about the role of love in marriage.

I remember you said that you dated for two years. Let me remind you of how much you loved each other. You told me that you practically saw each other every day. Your love for each other must be great. You did many things together: movies, shopping, restaurants, visiting friends and relatives, etc. I am wondering what has happened to your first love. Five years ago you exchanged your vows. It seems to me that your love and care for each other are dwindling. What can you do about it? I believe that was your question. You have to reflect on why you love and care for each other. You ought to remember your first love for each other. Your love is supposed to increase and you are supposed to care for each other more, even more than dating time. It is not too late. You can start all over again. Brad is still Brad, Amy is as beautiful as she was perhaps more beautiful than before your marriage.

You should test your love and care - why are they decreasing instead of increasing? Try to be honest with your individual self and with each other. You need to be frank with each other. Maybe the best way to do it is to find a third party. If you can find a Christian marriage counselor, it will be great. Otherwise, you can talk to your pastor and see if he will be able to help you. When love is missing, care will get lost, other important elements in marriage – commitment, trust, forgiveness, etc. - will also be scarce. You have to do whatever you can to find the love which got lost. Remember that the missing love is in your closet; part of it is in your bedroom. A big piece of it is in your mouths. You should not forget how many times you said, "I love you" while you were dating. What made you stop saying it? Or how many times do you say, "I love you" in a day, week, even in a month? Since you are still Brad and Amy who were so much in love during your dating, you are still the same persons. Bring your love back. Fall in love again. Do fun things together, find time for each other. Go away when necessary. Talk to each other meaningfully. Caress each other, it was unofficial during dating, now it is authentic; express your love to each other often. When each one of you is away, how many times do you say, "I miss you, honey, I can't wait to see you" when you call home.

Let things keep rolling again. Lift your love banner high. You can do it. No one can do it for you. Try to save your marriage and use your lifetime warranty giving by God. It is good for you and your children. Above all, talk to God; go to bible study group or prayer meetings together. Find time to read and study chapter thirteen of the first letter of St. Paul to the Corinthians. Test yourselves and each other on it. As Christ loves the church, Brad, you need to love Amy, and care of Brad is in your hand, Amy. Just do yourselves a favour, love each other. The God of love will give you desire to love and care for each other affectionately.

Dear Brad and Amy,

It is always good to talk to you on the phone. I am happy to know that you are improving on your love for each other. You are working hard to save your marriage. It's worth it. If love is there, the rest will follow gradually.

You want me to talk about commitment. It is a big subject/topic in marriage, because each one of you is committed to your work and your bosses, you always try your best to keep your job and impress your bosses to get promotions. You both have to drive to work for about 40 minutes each way to your workplaces. To be late to work is to invite trouble. I will believe that you are doing your best to be good workers. You try to take it easy with your managers and co-workers. Why are you doing all of these? Because you want to keep your jobs and you want to be good workers with good reputation.

It will be great if you can try to see the importance of commitment in your marriage as vital as your jobs, perhaps more paramount than your jobs. When you said, "I do" about six years ago, you were more than ready to go the extra mile to make it happen during dating. You have seen your commitment during your courtship grown, perhaps daily. You worked hard to make it happen. You are looking at the relationship you built up so high coming down gradually. It is not supposed to be like that, you know what? It is not too late for you to stop tearing down your commitment and continue rebuilding your relationship. . Rome was not built in a day. Don't stop building upon what you have started. Do not be discouraged. Slowly but surely, it will come if you do not give up.

May I suggest that you watch your wedding video again? Pay attention to the music, bible lessons, sermon and most importantly your vows. Count the number of times you kissed each other, especially while you were dancing. You can make every day your wedding day. Have your honeymoon over and over again and let it continue without end especially in your hearts. Let your house be the best hotel you can imagine, your bed can be your "honeymoon bed" each night – fall in love, tell each other his/her strength, what you admire in him/her with a promise that you will do your best to keep your marriage candle – love and all good things in your marriage – burning.

Christ committed himself to come to the world to die for you and me; he never looked back, even though it was not easy on him. He stood by his commitment, which took him to the cross. He did not regret his decision to come to the world to die for the sin of humanity. If he had to die all over again, he will do so as a criminal without any hesitation. He is able to help you to stand by your promise – commitment – to each other. He is the present help in time of trouble. May he be there for you and help you to be faithful to your commitment.

Dear Amy and Brad,

It's good to know that things are improving. You said that your sexual life is not as good as it had been. You will like me to advise you.

Even though you said you were doing great in your first two years of marriage. I am wondering what stole away your sexual relationship. For the past one year, you have been living almost like roommates- Brad had been going to bed late, and Amy you said sometimes you felt unmarried. You have also been thinking of having sexual intercourse somewhere else. You admitted that some of your friends are doing that and advised you to join them. Brad, this is a serious issue. Whatever is holding you from falling in love sexually, you need to deal with it. I wrote you before regarding your communication, your love for each other, and your commitment. However, all of these are coming along well. Since sexual intercourse is missing or is not good enough, you are not doing a good job. To be one body sexually means a lot in marriage. The two of you have to sit down and talk. Your seventh anniversary is on the way. You surely need to plan how to make your marriage better. Brad you should tell Amy why you have been going to bed late, why TV, movies and the computer are robbing your marriage of genuine relationship. Eight years ago, nothing could replace Amy's love in your life. Why now? Amy is still Amy. Amy, I hope that you are not refusing Brad his sexual needs or desires. Whatever the issue is or was - you need to talk about it and start a new page in your marital life.

Since you were joined together in marriage, nothing should separate you, even sex. You need to change your perspective with regards to sexual intercourse. God wants you to enjoy it that is one of the reasons he gave you to each other. Don't replace sexual love with other things; you have to satisfy each other sexually and otherwise. Your love for each other sexually and otherwise ought to be your focus in having a healthy martial relationship. Brad, verbally express God's beauty in Amy. Amy, try to see God's image in Brad. Tell each other how beautiful/handsome you are. Carry this positive affirmation to bed. No one can or should take or replace your love for each other. Brad, Amy is your woman, the most beautiful woman in the world. God gave you- both of you-to each other because he knows that you are good for each other, and that you will be able to satisfy each other sexually and otherwise. Don't make God a liar. He said; "it is not good for Brad to be alone, I will make a help mate, Amy, for him" (Gen. 2: 18). God has done his part, both of you have to do your part, too. Ask God to create in you, Brad, a thirst and hunger for Amy and Amy, you must tell God to implant Brad's desire in your life. We have enough divorces in the country; you don't need to join the statistics. Get back the enjoyment of your sexual intercourse from Satan. God bless you.

Dear Amy and Brad,

How wonderful it is to know that you have been going to bed together and that your sexual intercourse is improving. I thank God for helping you to adjust quickly.

In a month, you will celebrate your 7th wedding anniversary. The figure seven is a Godly figure. Seven represents God's perfection. God is good, perfect, and unique. God wants you and your marriage to be good, even perfect, and for your marriage to be unique. You can aim toward being a good couple. Perhaps you need to work on what can hold you back in your relationship. You don't need any set backs. Forward ever, backward never. In order to let this be in your marital life, you need to "let go." When we were talking on the phone last week, you raised the issue of past offences. So today, I want to talk about forgiveness. Because of bitterness, grudges, etc. many marriages have been ship wrecked. The idea of "my right" or "my marriage," is a choice that any serious husband/wife needs to make. If you want to embrace a "my right" attitude, a piece may be missing in your marriage, lack of forgiveness - hold on to my right. Any husband or wife may say; "I have the right to be angry, to hold on to my anger, to refuse talking to my partner, to even reject him/her from my life. I will never forgive him/her, it is over. I don't want anything to do with him/her again." These are the sentences/phrases you can hear from many bitter partners. I believe they are familiar to you. If you have this kind of attitude toward each other, I will like you to consider your marriage instead of "my right."

All unsolved issues should be dealt with as soon as possible. The more you prolong anger or bitterness, the more you damage your marital relationship. Each one of you needs to humble yourself before each other and ask for forgiveness. Don't feel too big to do so. Jesus taught us to forgive one another. In Matthew chapter 18:22, Jesus wants us to forgive one another 70x7; 490 times a day. What Jesus is teaching here is total forgiveness. Don't hold any grudge against each other. Do yourself a favour Brad, forgive Amy. For Brad, do the same, Amy. Perhaps you can take a weekend to go away to talk about all this stuff that may rob your marital joy or enjoyment. God wants you to be happy, to have joy, to have a good relationship. I, too, wish you the same. Make good use of God's lifetime warranty on your marriage. Talk to him, he will fix it for you.

Love heals the wounds of the past. God heals both the present and the past. God wants you to stay together in a good relationship. You should let go of the hurts incurred on each other and allow God to come into your marriage, that is, to be at the center of your home. Do not go to bed without talking about your grievances. Start each day together in the presence of God, read your bible in the morning and pray to God to help you to be Jesus for each other – that is what being a Christian means. Do what Christ would do, if he is there in your home. Tell your friends that you have asked God to help you and he did. Well, if I don't talk or write to you before your seventh anniversary, I wish you all the best. May God continue to demonstrate his power of forgiveness through you, be blessed in the Lord.

Dear Brad and Amy,

What good news Brad! Amy called me to share with me the news of your anniversary. You exchanged new rings and new vows/commitments. Second Honeymoon, wow!! You should testify to your friends who might be in the same boat for encouragement. God specializes in fixing what is broken. He can fix any broken home or marriage.

Let me talk to you about how to keep the ball rolling. God intended for your marriage to be stable. You need to work with him and follow His master plan for a stable marriage. God's intention is for marriage to last till a natural death of one of the couples. Any unstable marriage is in danger of a fight or a divorce. Brad and Amy, do your best to make your marriage stable.

Be aware of signs of crisis in your marital life. I have shared some of these signs with you: lack of effective communication, lack of commitment, infrequent sex or lack of satisfaction during sexual intercourse, lack of affection – love, (agape), unforgiving attitude, lack of trust, unfaithfulness, selfishness, poor money management, not sharing, how to handle expenses, in-laws, how to handle conflict, lack of adjustment, stubbornness to change, interference by old friends. All of these and others are killers of marriage. They can easily lead to divorce. And divorce is a killer. It has killed so many couples, even physically, through suicide. Don't walk closer to divorce. No one gains from divorce except lawyers. Children lose the most. Be careful, don't talk or think of divorce. Run away from it. Divorce is an enemy of your marriage, it is better to see it that way.

Find yourself a good group for Christian couples. If there is any bible study or prayer meeting group in your church or in your community, find your way there. Make Christ the unseen guest in your home. Let him be your marriage counselor all the time; remember the prophet Isaiah calls him a wonderful counselor. If he and the Holy Spirit are in your home, you will have peace, in fact, Christ is the prince of peace (Isaiah 9:6). He will give peace to you, joy, hope, and love will be yours, too. He was born for all; you in particular, to have rest of mind and stable life. Call on Christ all the time, he knows how to unload burdens and replace it with peace and rest (Matt. 11:28-30).

Continue the courting (dating) that you started during your second honeymoon – at your 7th anniversary. The Lord who has started a good work in your marriage will keep it till the end – when death should do you part 100 years to come, I hope. At any rate, thank you for allowing me to come into your marital life. Keep on dating, have fun all the time, share everything together – your body inclusive. I pray that God will bless you, your marriage, and the works of your hands.

Chapter 3
Bob & Sarah – Cheating on Marital Partner

Dear Bob and Sarah,

It was a good marriage seminar as you said on the phone the other day. My wife and I liked it, too; there was a lot of sharing and information.

I would like to thank you for the confidence you have in me to share your marital struggles with me. I know what you were saying, I can sense what you said Bob that Sarah was unfaithful to you for about two years. It must be hurting. I believe her boss must also be having problems with his wife. But the good news is that Sarah admitted her faults. Sarah, I hope it is over with your boss. Have you told him that your husband knows about the two-year affair? If you have not told him, the first step for Bob's healing is for him to know that you, Sarah and your boss have stopped and that it is not to continue. Perhaps Sarah, you may be wondering what will happen to your job, if you refuse to continue the extra-marital affair with him. He needs to know that he has no right to fire you from your job. If he does or starts to treat you unfairly, you have the right to report him to the higher authority at your workplace. If you have not told him, it will be a good idea for you to do so. This will be a good beginning of mending a broken relationship. I will be interested to know how you (Sarah) make out with your boss. But you have to make sure that it is over indeed, no matter what. Promise Bob and yourself that you will be faithful to your marital vows.

Both of you, Bob and Sarah find time to talk and be open with each other. Try to avoid blaming each other. Why was Sarah unfaithful to you, Bob, and what went wrong in your relationship? Even though Sarah told me that you were unable to satisfy her sexually and that your love for her was questionable, and she tried to find someone she thought would be able to show her love and meet her sexual needs. Bob, you, too, said that Sarah is spending more time with her friends, and comes home late. You need to talk over all issues like these and remove the cog from the wheel of your marital progress.

You need to find out what happened to your love and consider the possibility of bringing it back and making it even stronger than before. You have shared with me how you used to do things together like going out to eat at least two times a week and traveling during your vacation time. You may be thinking that those days are gone but you can continue on with these activities, even making them better than before. I believe you can do it. Just find a good time to talk. Perhaps you could go away for one weekend to avoid any interruptions. We will talk about how you can warm up your cold relationship. Nine years ago, your love for each other was so strong. It can happen again. Talk, be open, and be ready to let go and let God. If you can invite God in your discussion, it will be great. I believe God has been expecting a time like this to come into your marital life. God hates divorce. I hope you will try to hate it also. May God help you to be sincere, and honest with yourselves, God bless you.

Dear Bob and Sarah,

I was so delighted to hear that you had a wonderful weekend last week and that you were able to sort things out. You both admitted your faults without much controversy. Good job.

Your next step now is forgiveness and reconciliation. You ought to forgive each other and yourselves - self-forgiveness. It is not easy, but if you truly want your good old days back, you should forgive each other and yourselves (individually). Let me tell you a true story of a couple. They were married for about fifteen years. In the meantime, the wife started to sleep with her husband's best friend; one day, the secrets were exposed. The husband felt betrayed, disappointed and angry. They both found time to talk, the wife cried and asked for forgiveness. Even though it was hurtful on the part of the husband, but he did forgive his wife. They learned from their mistakes, they prayed together and started a new life. To turn into a new page in marital life is to try to forget about yesterday.

Forgive and forget seem to be an old tradition in our modern marital life. If one realizes his/her mistakes, it is the job of the other partner to accept him/her back and try to forget the past. God the founder of the institution of marriage knew what sin and forgiveness are. He is always ready to forgive sinners and wash him/her totally with the blood of Jesus Christ, his son and to start a new life. Isaiah says: "Come now, let us reason together," says the Lord, "though your sins are like scarlet, they shall be as white as snow; though they are red as crimson, they shall be like wool. If you are willing and obedient, you will eat the best from the land" (Isaiah 1:18-19) (NIV). God is full of forgiveness. Bob needs to be like God with regards to forgiveness, and if there are some hurts in you, too, Sarah, you should forgive Bob and bring back joy into your marriage, peace, love, hope, happiness, fun, enjoyment, care, commitment, good communication, oneness, unity, friendship etc. I believe you can do it. You have done the most difficult aspect of how to be happy again. If you truly forgive each other and become friends again- happy couple- verse 19 of Isaiah chapter I will be fulfilled in your marriage, that is, you will eat the best from the land, which will be the best of your home. You will be able to see together your children getting married, have their own families and all of you will be happy together.

I will encourage you to study your bible together. Try to begin each day with the Lord. Pray each morning before you go to work. Pray for each other and for your children, Joe and Josh. You ought to pray also to God to help you to let go of hurts and help you to love each other as you ought to. Remember, forgiveness is necessary in your marriage. Because of bitterness, many couples had seen the pre mature death of their marriages. God want your marriage to last and for both of you to celebrate many good things with your children, grandchildren and great-grandchildren, may it be so for you. Be good, God loves you, he cares for you, he cares for you and your marriage, too and so do I

Dear Bob and Sarah,

Yes, Sarah, that is how it is supposed to be! You have put an end to your relationship with your boss. I hope he, too, would find a way to confess to his wife and ask for forgiveness, but it is up to him. Whenever you have one on one discussion or business with him, be careful. If he wants to win you back, pray to God to give you strength to resist temptation. Let Bob continue to have faith and trust in you.

It is not easy to establish trust again. But guess what? It is possible. Old things can easily rob us of a good relationship with God or each other. When the apostle Paul says: "Therefore, if anyone is in Christ, he is a new creation; the old has gone, the new has come" (II cor. 5:17) (NIV). Paul the apostle was right. If a bad behavior is gone from a person, he or she is a new person. On the part of Sarah, you need to continue to be a new Sarah and Bob should not see old Sarah but new Sarah. You, Bob, should try to trust new Sarah as long as new is still new. Don't see old in the new. Try to trust new Sarah. This is what God does for us, as long as we turn our lives over to him in the way of seeking forgiveness. He established faith and confidence in us. He trusts us and believes in us. We ought to do the same for each other and one another. So try to establish a stronger belief and trust in each other. Since you have used your God's lifetime warranty to restore your relationship, whenever the devil tries to remind you of the past, tell him that you are no longer dwelling in the past; you a person or persons of present and future.

Joe and Josh must have been very glad that the atmosphere in the house has changed. They trust you that you can do it and that their lives which have been entrusted into your hands by God will be saved. I will believe they don't want a dead home. They want a happy home, a loving home full of peace and harmony. Let them- your children- continue to see a new marriage, a new hope and new parents in you. Love never fails. When love fails, trust is in a serious danger. In order for your trust to be alive and active, you need to activate your love for each other. It is a great commitment to love and trust each other in marriage. It should be your new endeavor to care for each other, to seek not just what will make you, Bob and Sarah, happy individually, but what will help you to share happiness together. You are no more two since you said "I do" about ten years ago. If there is any doubt in any of you, quickly talk about it. A good communication will tighten your trust and your marital relationship. I will be talking more on the importance of effective communication.

As I said before, allow God in your marriage, commit each day into his hands. Do not worry about your tomorrow, "one day at a time." That is what you surely need. God will bless you with a strong faith in each other which will boost your trust in each other and your relationship. You can do it. Try to cooperate with God. He is able to do for you more than you can ever imagine. May he help you, uphold you and keep you, your children and marriage safe. Amen.

Dear Bob and Sarah,

As I promised that I will be talking more about communication. At the same time, it is good that you are doing fine and that your trust is coming back gradually. I am happy for you and your children, and thank you for your kind words in the card you sent to me. My joy is to see you moving forward. I believe you can do it.

Communication is one of the keys to successful marriage. Couples may say," we communicate," but how effective is their communication? Bob and Sarah, some years ago, I agreed to pick up my daughter from a camp and to drive a girl from American side of the border. I told her mom that we would be in the house at 2:00 pm. We got to their home at 1:45 pm. I told the girls that "Mrs. Johnson" (not her real name) would be home soon. Two o'clock came and past. I started to wonder what was going on. I thought she was just late for few minutes but she did not arrive until 2:45 pm. She was happy and said, "I made it." I interrupted, "made what?" She replied; "this is 1:45 pm." I argued; "no, it is 2:45." Yes, she was right, it was 1:45pm American, zone time and 2:45 pm my time. I communicated with Mrs. Johnson (not her real name), but it was not a good communication – an effective communication supposed to be 2:00 pm my time. I assumed that she should know that I was talking about my time and she also thought I was talking of her time. You can see that I wasted the girls' time and mine because of lack of effective communication. Let your communication be effective and stop making assumptions. Ask questions when necessary.

A lack of effective communication can bring a big disaster into a marital relationship. Talk clearly to each other, even to your children. Don't think they understand or they're supposed to understand, each one of you need to ask questions, if the idea or communication is not clear enough. Listen carefully and attentively, when you are communicating with each other. It will be a good idea, when you are talking about an important matter, to make sure your TV, or radio is not on. It will not be good to be working on a computer or any other thing that can interfere with or divide your attention.

God is our example with regard to communication. Jesus Christ represents him very well. He used parables, but later on, he gave the interpretation of the parables. If you are joking, let your partner know what you are saying is a joke. Call upon Christ to teach you how to enjoy your communication. He is able to help you more than you can think. Communication with compassion – have who you are talking with in mind – so highly needed in any serious couple who wants to make their marriage work or better. Care for each other, care for your children and above all, love and care for your marriage. If you want to save your time at the end of the day, spend time to communicate effectively, to avoid apologizing in the evening. God wants you to communicate effectively with him, too. Make your marriage desires known to him. He will not only listen to you, he will act as soon as possible.

Dear Sarah and Bob,

Wow! You went to Cuba for your 10th anniversary. That was great. I am happy for you. So you had a good time, you were able to talk over so many issues. You had a lot of romantic times. You needed such badly, and I am happy you treated yourselves as a new couple. The Cuba trip reminds you of your honeymoon ten years ago, I guess. Nothing was stopping you before – for the past years- from enjoying each other and treating each other as a "King and Queen." God calls you a very good, dependable couple. He wants the best for you, and I am glad that you see your marriage as God sees it- God is always positive about your marital life, he sees a lot of potential in your marriage; growth, health, mutual understanding, unity etc.

I will like to encourage you to continue to water what you have planted 10 years ago, it was almost dead, but you fertilized it in Cuba. It seems to be growing well now. All you need to do is water it regularly. Do you get what I'm saying? The vow you made at your wedding, you almost forgot it, but you reminded yourselves and you renewed it. You should try now to see it working. It can, I believe. Many marriages survive 60 years plus. In fact, I know some couples who have made it up to 75 years. I'm not joking. If some can do it with God's help, you can do it, too. God is interested in a long healthy marriage for you. Remind each other and yourselves individually about your commitment to your marriage and to each other. During "ups" and "downs" don't run away. Tough times don't last, tough couples do. You need to ask God to give you an understanding heart – both of you – and also a humble heart to be able to learn from each other, listen to each other and above all learn from God.

I don't need to remind you of your past, but I don't want it to come back to you. Go to bed together, when it is possible. Give your body to each other. Do your best to enjoy one of the fundamentals of marriage – I hope you know what I'm talking about, sex. You cannot replace it with something else. God created it, because he created marriage. Enjoy it to the best of your ability. Both of you should make sure that you enjoy it personally and mutually. Have it as often as you both want it. Do not overwork yourselves every night to make unnecessary excuses. Remember, I wrote about communication. Sex, touching, kissing, romance in general are non-verbal communication which any healthy marriage must have, which means you need both verbal and non-verbal communication. Both must be done well-effective communication. Read to or write good poems for each other – find good Christian books on that. The book of Songs of Solomon in the bible is good. Proverbs 31:10-31 is one of the best for you. Bob, read it to Sarah to let her know that she is a noble wife of yours. Always express to each other; you're beautiful/handsome, the best wife/husband, and a great mom/dad – on behalf of your children. I know those scripture excerpt will be an encouraging sayings that can make each one of you feel good. Strive to be the best – wife/husband to your optimum ability. Give me a call or email or write me anytime. I will try to be there for you. Be blessed in the name of the Lord.

Chapter 4
Jake & Judy – When the Last Child Leaves Home for College

Dear Jake and Judy,

I do not mind to be talking to you through letters. I am glad that your friends Brad and Amy told you about me. I am glad they did. I enjoyed our phone conversation the other day.

You both said that you have been having marital problems for a while. Judy, I asked you why you want a separation now, and you said that you have been waiting for your last child to leave home for college. She has finally gone to college and you think you should now put an end to your marriage. You both agreed that your children knew about the situation in your marriage and at home in particular. Your children were crying when they were told about your decision. Why were they crying? Since they knew about the unhealthy and nasty marriage you have, I will guess they were trying to blame themselves for leaving, since you have been managing for all those years. They may ask, "Why now?" especially Kathy, who just left home. Kathy may be thinking; "my mom is leaving home because I left home for college."

Jake had been cheating on you for some years by having affairs with his secretary and one of your friends. It must have hurt you so badly. To be sexually unfaithful is not fair. Jake, I am wondering if you ever put yourself in Judy's shoes. That is, if Judy was sexually unfaithful to you, how would you feel? Even though Jake, you said, you are not a husband in your room, because Judy feels she is getting old sexually because she is forty seven. You were not happy with the way Judy had been treating you, and I am wondering, if you were trying to get her back for refusing you as her husband in your bed. Thus, making you more or less like roommates.

Judy, you should be thinking beyond cheating, and Jake also needs to see himself as a husband anywhere, including your room. What I think is lacking in your marriage is love. Your love is getting old as you think your marriage is. Your love is getting cold. You need to warm it up. Is it too late? Maybe not, however, to bring your first love back, you will need to cooperate with me, and to be sincere with yourselves and your marriage. You don't necessarily need to restore your marriage just because of your children, but for the two of you. You will need to reflect, improve your communication and do something about your commitment to your marriage. It is not too late to fall in love again. You just have to start all over. Remember, during your dating and early years of your marriage, I believe that you were indeed absolutely in love. If I am correct, think of what made you love each other so dearly and try to relive them. You have to let go of what is dividing you and go for what has worked for your unity, and the love, care, and support you had for each other. Your children are hurting. You don't really need to worry about that now, just think of what action you need to take and implement it. I believe you told me which church you attend. Start going there together again; pray to God to guide you in your decision and your communication. Do it for Jake and Judy. Keep in touch. God bless you.

Dear Jake and Judy,

Thank you for your emails, letters and phone calls. You have been talking about the problems you've been having in your marriage. That is a good start. Knowing the problems is good but doing something about it is much better.

Jake you have done a good job for the courage you had to take a risky step by telling your secretary and the other woman that "it's over." Those women's look out is how to deal with their husbands regarding their extra-marital affairs. The issue between the two of you is how to find a solution to the problem. Judy, since you have agreed to give Jake a second chance, in fact, that is a good idea. Our God is a God of many chances, you need to be patient with Jake and try to allow trust and confidence in him to be back gradually. You both must adjust your ways and allow change in your relationship. It seems impossible to have a big change in a short time, yet it is possible. Do not rush, but be open always to both adjustments and change. Our Lord Jesus Christ is unchangeable Changer. If you can consult him, he will help you to work on the healings and to change things around for the best.

Both of you had allowed the flesh to control your marriage instead of the Holy Spirit. If you can allow the Holy Spirit to control your marriage, you will experience; love, joy, peace, patience, kindness, goodness, faithfulness, gentleness and self-control and also you will be able to crucify the sinful nature with its passions and desires. In contrast, if the works of the flesh are still lurking somewhere; something like sexual immorality, impurity, hatred, discord, jealousy, fits of rage, selfish ambition, factions and envy may like to control your marital life (Galatians 5:16-24). I will encourage you to let go of the flesh in your minds and also in your marriage. Give God a chance to be in charge of your marriage. He is the one who instituted it. He must know how to fix it. He is the best marriage fixer. Any purchased item with warranty can be returned for repair so also you can make use of God's lifetime warranty in your marriage. I know your marriage is broken, the trust is gone. Love had been replaced with hatred and anger. It is natural. The wound is deep enough, no one to fill up the hole. As I said before, prayer will not only change things around for you, but it will change you. If each one of you can change for better, you will treat each other as you would like to be treated. What you would not like Jake to do to you Judy, refrain from it, and vice versa, Jake.

When you are ready for a change and adjustments and allow the Spirit of God to rule and control your life, then it will be easier to let go of the hurts or wounds. Even before one says; "I am sorry, please forgive me," the other will be more than ready to forgive. This will turn your marriage around for better. Your children and couples or people around will not need to be told. They will notice it, and verbalize it to you and be talking about it among themselves. Well, if you still want me to talk about forgiveness and letting go, I will be happy to do so. Keep in touch. Be good to each other, demonstrate love to and care for each other as God in Christ Jesus does to you. Be blessed in the Lord.

Dear Jake and Judy,

I am delighted to know that you have been working hard on forgiveness. You have told each other that you were sorry and ready to let go. Since you have asked God to help you to forgive and forget, he is able to do so. He is unchangeable changer. He doesn't want any couples to graduate from the marriage institution that he inaugurated. He wants the best for you and your marriage.

You wanted me to talk about what you need to do next. It is very simple. Try to forget the past, let go, let God. You should stop doing whatever you think your partner will not be happy with. Those things that were hurting your marriage need to be abandoned. Let people at work know that you are married and that you love and like your wife/husband. Tell your co-workers good stuff about each other, nothing negative should be said to any of your friends. Whenever you start to discuss bad things about your spouse, you are inviting wrong counseling; in most cases- from opposite sex co-workers who may say: "I will never allow my husband/wife to do that to me," Perhaps they are trying to let you know that they are interested in you and that they are not happy with their marriage partners. So you have to be careful of what you say and whom you say it to. In other words, if you don't have any good thing to say about each other to your friends or co-workers, it is better not to say anything.

Refrain from any attitude that will irritate your partner. Try to be nice to each other. As you are trying to let go of your past, try to do what each one of you think Jesus would do to his spouse, if he were you. You are not only Christians, but you are ambassadors of Jesus to each other and to people around you. As God through Jesus Christ has forgiven you, do the same to each other. "Come now, let us reason together," says the Lord, "though your sins are like scarlet, they shall be as white as snow, though they are red as crimson they shall be like wool" (Isaiah 1:18) (NIV). This invitation of God's forgiveness to sinners is for you, me and others. Since he has forgiven you and washed you in the blood of Jesus Christ, you are now being restored to him. The hurts you inflicted on each other are part of what God washed away by the blood of his son, Jesus Christ. Our sins were "red," so many and great, yet God forgave us. Thus, as God has forgiven you, you should forgive yourself and each other. And do not try to bring the memory back. Forgive each other and God is able to wash you as white as snow. That is total forgiveness; Isaiah 1:19 says, "if you are willing and obedient, you will eat the best from the land." That is, if you can forgive each other and obey God's command, you will see the betterment of your marriage. You will be happy again. You will be able to see your grandchildren and great-grand-children together. God loves and cares for you and I do, too. Keep fit in the Lord. Keep in touch.

Dear Jake and Judy,

I am glad to hear, from our phone conversation, that you are no longer dwelling in the past and trying to move on. Good job, Judy and Jake. The apostle Paul said it rightly, "therefore, there is now no condemnation for those who are in Christ Jesus" (Romans 8:1) (NIV). You have taken a good step. Jake, you confessed to Judy and asked for forgiveness. Judy, you did the same. You have forgiven each other and prayed to God to forgive you. You have been forgiven. I could remember that you said your Pastor knew about the whole episode and prayed for you also. Great!! You are a new "creation." You are just like a new couple. As Paul the apostle said in 1 Corinthians 5:17, "Therefore, if anyone is in Christ, he is a new creation; the old has gone, the new has come!" (NIV).

The only old thing about your marriage that you should remember is your dating and the early years of your marriage. Try not to remember the old - when things were of the world with regard to your marriage. If the devil wants to remind you of the past, just tell him that you are older than that. You are older than allowing the past to control you or your marriage because you are in Jesus Christ.

Since you have been doing so much better, I will encourage you to spend more time together and communicate effectively. Share your burdens together, even work problems; couples should be there for each other. Sharing is very important; share your concerns, your fear, your pain and joy together. Since none of your children is at home, you should spend plenty of time together in the evenings and on weekends. Talk, laugh, and watch good movies or news on the TV together. Going to bed together, holding hands, touching here and there means a lot in marital life.

Do not forget that you are not too old, in my opinion, to enjoy each other through sexual intercourse. Verbal and non-verbal communications are essential. Do not neglect one for the other. Communication will help you deal with many issues that could accumulate to cause disintegration in your relationship. Find time to iron things out, talk and talk until you reach a compromise. Do not give the devil a stronghold. Refrain from debates, faultfinding, and control or manipulation; focus more on reconciliation through mutual understanding. Share your insight for your future and your dreams for your children. Ask questions when and where necessary during your conversation.

I am delighted to know that you have been sharing your marriage turn-around experience with your friends and co-workers. I am also pleased that your Pastor, during the Sunday service, asked you to share how it happened and where you now are in your marital life. I believe you will continue to grow stronger in faith, love, care, support and hope together. It is good that you are giving peace, marital joy and happiness a chance in your relationship. Continue to let God guide and lead you in all your ways. Talk to God together in prayer and study his word together. He has many surprises for you and many good things for you to celebrate together.

I wish you all the best in your upcoming anniversary. Reach out to many couples who are having tough times. God bless you beyond measure.

Dear Jake and Judy,

Congratulations on your 27th wedding anniversary. It must be a big celebration. Your Pastor came to your house, while all your children came home for the celebration. You reaffirmed your vows and commitment – how wonderful! I was thrilled to find out that you were able to share the testimony of your turn around story. You have done a great job in saving your marriage in a remarkable way. You are a living example to many young couples, including your own children.

I am hoping you will be able to have some time together with your children to explain to them how things turned around for you. It will be nice, if you can also try to apologize to them for the bad experience they went through. It will be a good learning process for all the children. It would be good if you could have small-scale seminars around your city for couples experiencing what you went through. Many couples have lost hope, some want a way out of their marital ordeal, but they don't know how. You will be a good resource couple for them.

Pray about it and if you need any help, let me know. I will not mind to give you some resources on marriage enrichment. Talk to your pastor and ask him to pray with you. I, too, will join you in prayer. It has been a pleasure to know you and to be talking to you for the past two years. I hope you will not mind me to make reference to your story when necessary? You were so easy to work with. I learnt a lot from you. Thank you for your trust and willingness to share. Since you are not solely relying on your ability to work things out by yourselves, I believe that the Lord who has been supporting you, and has helped you to calm the big marital storm is able to sustain, uphold and glue you together until the day of the Lord or till death do you a part.

I do hope that things will continue to be great with you and that all good things will come your way. Feel free to call or e-mail me. I would like to pray with you; Lord Jesus, I thank you for Jake and Judy. Thank you for their big marital renewal. Thank you for their love and fear for you. I pray that you uphold them as long as both of them shall live. Let your Holy Spirit lead them day-by-day to be a couple after your own heart. Be with them as they tell other couples about their marital rejuvenation. Give them all they need to represent you. Bless their children. Help them to continue to be faithful to you, to each other and to their family. Thank you again for your love toward them, in Jesus name. Amen

Chapter 5
Vince & Anna – A Couple with Sons who Abuse Drugs And Alcohol

Dear Vince and Anna,

It was nice talking to you the other week. As I promised, I am writing about your son, John's situation that has been causing tension between the two of you for almost two years. When we spoke, you said that he spends more time hanging out with his friends than he does at home, drinks heavily, and uses drugs. You also mentioned that you are not sure, if he will be able to graduate from high school because he was suspended for fighting.

Since you have been unable to reach a compromise regarding how to deal with the issue, I will suggest that you try your best to be one again. As the saying goes, "united we stand, divided we fall." Both of you need to tackle this problem together. The matter is bigger than what only one person can handle. I know you have tried talking with him, blaming him, fighting him and sometimes rejecting him.

Anna, you always disagree whenever Vince says that John cannot come in and does not open the door for him around 3:00am. You also find it difficult to say no to John when he asks for money. Both of you are right - for Vince to say no and Anna to say yes. One thing you need to know is- until you have a common denominator - stand on the same level, have the same voice and reach a compromise as to how to deal with John - he may continue to play game. It must be definitely frustrating and straining on your relationship, to see the oldest of your three sons exhibiting such behaviours.

Are you afraid that John is being a bad role model to his brothers? His brothers are observing you, so be very careful because the steps you take to deal with him are very crucial. You need peace and harmony because children like to see division between their parents so that they will be able to manipulate and separate them through their actions. Both of you need to discipline yourselves and try to show tough love. Mike, your second son, has started to come home late nightly during the week, smokes occasionally and likes to dress like his brother. It can become a serious issue, if you do not take radical steps to curb your children's behaviours.

The Guidance counselor at school has spoken with John and Mike and has had little impact on Mike and no success with John. As I mentioned, the first step to be taken is for both of you to be united and have one voice so that the children cannot capitalize on your division. When A says no, B must cooperate, by so doing it will be easier to help the children, especially John. The second step is to show genuine love to them, John in particular - let him know that you love him unconditionally. Talk less with them, don't judge them, try to accommodate them, but you have to be frank and firm. Let them know that you don't tolerate what they are doing. You don't need to say it all the time, but whenever you want to say it, use the word "we" instead of "I." It will be nice to specify to John that both of you are talking, even, if only one of you is with him. Another step to take is prayer. I will be talking more about this in my next letter, you cannot change John, but God can. Before you get my next missive, try the first two steps and let us see how things turn out. My prayers are with you.

Dear Vince and Anna,

Thank you for your kind words spoken during our conversation on the phone. I am happy that you have stopped arguing. You have been saying and doing things together with your boys. Anna, John has stopped coming to you to ask for money because you have been telling him to go ask his dad any time he asks you for money. Good job! Continue to work as a team, stand on what you believe and transmit it well to your boys, especially John. Try to keep hope alive. It is possible for John to come back to his senses. Don't lose hope, even regarding his education. A major turnaround is possible. You should minimize your conversation with him each time and pray more for him. Remember what is impossible with you is so easy with God. The power of prayer is greater than anything in the whole universe.

The author of prayer is a person that we can count on. He said to call upon him and will answer us and show us great and mighty things. In the light of this promise, an uncountable number of people have had their prayers answered both in the bible and in real life. Think about Jabez, Hezekiah and others in the bible.

The devil knows that prayer is designed for his defeat. That is why he always hinders people from praying and even causes many who pray to doubt. He distracts others by making their minds wander or reminds them of what they have to do and other things like those. Prayer is a must for anyone who wants to be who God wants him/her to be. God cannot impose himself on anyone because he gave this world to us humans to manage. Before he can interfere in anyone's affairs, he must be invited through prayer. To walk in freedom, which Christ brought through his suffering and death, you must know who you are. God is in Jesus, you are in Jesus; Jesus and God are in you.

Now you can see that John needs to be viewed through the eyes of God. Remember the story of the prodigal son. His parents, especially the father kept on hoping for his return. I believe, his father was praying for him. There was a divine intervention and the son came to his senses and went back home. His father was so glad to see him and there was a great celebration (Luke 15: 11-32). John's situation is not as bad as that of the prodigal son. The unconditional love demonstrated by the father is what John needs. He doesn't need any judgment, condemnation, and criticism. Try to accept him just as he is and help him by letting him know that you love him. While you are doing your own part, continue praying to the one who promise to do whatever we ask for in prayer. I am so excited because John's matter is in God's hand and He can change his life in a twinkling of an eye.

God is the one who promised to give us a heart to obey him and that is John's portion. John will need to change his friends and you need find a way to pass that across to him. If he wants to talk to a counselor, you can find him a good one in your city. If you cannot find any one that you trust, you can encourage him to give me a call. I will see what I can do to help him.

What you need most for John is prayer. Tell God what you want for him, pray in his room every day, over his bed when he's not home. I have advised other parents to do the same thing and God answered their prayers and I did the same for a wayward child of mine, and God was faithful. He will surprise you by turning John's life around. Keep in touch. I promise you my prayers.

Dear Vince and Anna,

It was wonderful to talk to John on the phone a couple of days ago. He told me how much he has changed. He said he got admission into a university. I am so glad for you that he is doing great. He informed me that he attended a youth retreat in another city that transformed his life. He seemed to like it. I asked him about his brother, Mike, and he said that he's working with him. He gave me the impression that Mike is not doing badly. According to John, Mike did well on his Grade 10 report card.

Since you were able to patiently win John back to your side, I believe you can do the same with Mike. You are blessed because John is so supportive of you working on Mike. Do not worry about Mike, the Lord that set John free is still on the throne to do the same for Mike; He does not change and his kingdom has no end. Always remember that nothing is too difficult for him. Continue to pray as God wants us to make our request known to him. He is able and his powerful hands are strong enough to reform Mike. Do not be disappointed in him and do not use that words, "we or I'm disappointed in you or I hate you." You can say: "We love you, but we hate your actions or what you are doing."

Continue to encourage him to do well at school and to focus on what matters most. He has only been suspended from school once this semester and it was twice by this time last semester. Praise him for that and encourage him to do better in Grade 11. It would also be better if he replaces his current friends with ones who will have better influence on him.

Before John goes to College, make sure that he shares how he overcame his addiction and his bad experiences with Mike - such information can help him. John should also encourage him to put more effort into his studies and to limit his party attendance. However, the most important role you need to play in his life is to be there for him. Do not reject or abandon him. Check on him from time to time about what is going on in his life, not for monitoring purposes, but to know how to help out. Try to avoid jumping to conclusions on any issue and don't be judgmental. Try to be as friendly as possible.

You should also consider fasting so that you pray for him with much seriousness. You can start by skipping one meal per day and then you can gradually skip two. The latter (going without food until supper time) is the most common type of fasting. When you fast, you will be able to focus more on God to grant your request for Mike. Commit Mike to God and remember that God specializes in making the impossibility possible. We cannot force any change on our children, but God knows how to touch their hearts and let his will be done in their lives.

You can also remind Mike about the possible outcome of his wrong choices. Continue to invite him to family prayer time, pray for him relentlessly, do not judge or blame him. Love him unconditionally. Plan with him about his future; tell him that God's love for him is not based on his performance, but that the love of God is based on who he is. Continue to sow the seed of God's Word; it is bound to bring transformation into Mike's life. May God give you wisdom to deal with him.

Dear Anna and Vince,

The Lord is so good indeed. John has completed a year of university. I'm glad that He did very well in his courses. John's girlfriend seems to have great influence on him. It's great that they belong to a Christian group in the college and found a good church off Campus. His progress has been remarkable.

John called me about two months ago to share the latest development in his life with me and to tell me about Mike's big turnaround due to what happened to him more than six months ago. His story was similar to what you told me about Mike's arrest for drug possession during a police raid in their school. He ended up in Police custody for couple of hours and was suspended from school for one week, and ordered to write a letter of apology promising that he would not take drugs to school again. He did so and gave you a copy, then wrote you a different one pledging never to touch drugs again. He apologized to you and for the past six months, he has stopped using drugs and drinking alcohol. This is really incredible news!

You have witnessed that God's pathway for John's freedom was different from Mike's. God used John's girlfriend to overcome his bad habit while he used a serious scenario for Mike to discontinue with his reckless life. The basic thing is they both quit their bad habits. You must be extremely happy and thankful to see God in action. He is good, a refuge in time of trouble and answers those who diligently seek him. I am glad that your efforts were not in vain. Your expectations became a reality. I hope you will not stop there. Two of your three sons became substance abusers and are now free. There are many parents like you in your city, across the nation and around the world. I hope you will do whatever you can to help other parents whose children are in bondage of drugs and alcohol. Pray about it and think of what you can do to help out.

Maybe Mike's school will be a good place to start. He still has one year to finish. It is okay to work with the school administrators to organize a support group for parents who do not know the way out of their children's predicament. Check around to see if there are couples like you in your neighborhood or church who will be interested in starting a support group to learn a step by step approach to rescuing their children from the grips of drugs and alcohol. You never know how many can be touched through you. Talk with your Pastor about it and with your prayer and bible study groups. I assume that you will get positive response from them. You should not keep quiet in a time like this. For sure, Mike will be able to talk with his "buddies" at school or wherever his testimony is needed. He knows the language, he can go an extra mile to witness to the drug dealers in school and also give a testimony in his school assembly.

He shouldn't relent in his efforts, to seize any available opportunity, to speak about his freedom from drug and alcohol to those who have been enslaved as he was before. Many parents are crying because of their children's bad choices. I don't need to remind you because you have been there. They need you to help show them the way out. I will join you in prayers for courage and guidance with regard to what to do and how to do it. God is able to give you all you need. Experience is the best teacher and you have it. God bless you. Keep in touch.

Dear Vince and Anna,

I am thrilled to know about the wonderful job that the two of you and Mike are doing. You have started monthly support groups for the parents of drugs and alcohol addicts in your church as well as in Mike's high school. As you mentioned, the turnout is always great in both places; up to 40 at the church and 50 at the school. I am not surprised that you are having a good record of attendance. I'm happy that Mike was given the opportunity to give a testimony at school and at the church. You must be proud of Mike. God has brought out something beautiful out of an ugly circumstance.

Is it okay to take another step? It will be great, if both of you and Mike can find time to go and talk to the school's superintendent and share Mike's story with him/her as well as about the growth of the support group in your school. Try to encourage him or her to spread it to all high schools. Who knows, the answer may be yes which means the program can become widespread in the province. Someday, the good news will eventually extend across the country. If the superintendent hesitates to say yes, don't be discouraged. You may talk to the school principal to implore him or her and share the transformation being experienced through the group and Mike's evidence of the authenticity of the group. I hope it will work out for you. Before you go to the superintendent you can go to other schools in your city and solicit their consent as a necessity for allowing the program to expand.

God is able to win your high school and your city on his side through you. Don't worry about how God is going to do it. One school at a time, he is able to establish a support group across the nation. Parents whose children are going through the agony of drugs and alcohol abuse will appreciate your efforts to see their children being set free. At the same time, they will learn how to cope, while their children are going through the journey of recovery. Ask your Church – your Pastor in particular - to be praying for you. Nothing is impossible with God (Luke 1:37). Do not underestimate the power of God. God is able to work with you, and change many young people. Some of them are using drugs and consuming alcohol because they lack unconditional love in their lives. Share what you have learnt about winning your children on your side. Some parents are so judgmental and some are very critical of their children because of their frustration. It will be your job to educate parents on how to love unconditionally and to let love supersede criticism and judgment.

Mike's turned around award (usually given to any student who change from unproductive life to a better life) should be acknowledged by me – congratulations to both of you and him. The award needs to be one of the elements to be mentioned whenever you talk to a new group or the Superintendent. Both John and Mike's situations occurred so that you will be able to associate with the unchanging changer – God, to change many young people for the best. God will equip you for the task. Keep in touch. God bless you.

Chapter 6
Rob & Jane – A Couple With
An Alzheimer Parent

Dear Rob and Jane,

Greetings, it was nice to talk to you the other day. As you mentioned, Jane's mom has Alzheimer's disease. Jane is the only child of her parents and her dad passed on a couple of years ago. Jane, you promised your dad that you would take good care of your mom. Your mom can no longer live by herself and she does not want to go to a nursing home. You tried hard before you persuaded her to move in with you. Her situation is now getting worse and her doctor told you that she will not get better. Having Jane's mom live with you has caused tension between the two of you. This is your first major conflict in your 40 years plus of marriage.

The two of you have been experiencing challenges in caring for Jane's 88-year-old mother since she moved in with you. Moreover, it is difficult for the two of you as you are both ageing as well, with Rob being 67 years old and Jane being 65. I am wondering if you need to consider hiring a caregiver to relieve you sometimes. During the hours the caregiver is there, you will be able to have your life and do things you want to do. Think about it and look for someone good, who will be patient with your mom. The two of you need to try to make yourselves comfortable. Rob, you should not be frustrated. You have to remember, too, that you are no longer young. You need to enjoy your life and your retirement. I am wondering if you are concerned that Jane may also get Alzheimer's since her grandmother also had Alzheimer's disease. Is this concern adding to your frustrations? Guess what? Whatever the thought you have, you don't need to die before death. What you need to do is take it easy. One day at a time. You need to deal with each situation as it comes. Deal with Mrs. Brown's (Jane's mom), case as it comes. Do not be overwhelmed by the situation. Try to keep Mrs. Brown comfortable and at the same time, do not over do things; you yourselves need to do things in a way that your children will not be afraid of your future. Let your request be made known to God. Pray with and for Mrs. Brown. She is still able to recite Psalm 23 and the Lord's Prayer. Allow her to do that as often as possible. Remember to cast all your anxieties upon God, for he cares for you (Psalm 55:22; I Peter 5:7). I will be thinking of you.

Dear Rob & Jane,

Compliments of the day to you. Thank you for your note. Rob, you noted that you are frustrated not only because Jane is worn-out from taking care of her mom, but also because you fear the unknown regarding the perpetuation of the disease. You always worry about who is going to be the next patient. I don't blame you for thinking that way considering that Jane's grandmother and aunt also had Alzheimer's. You are wondering what is going to happen to Jane and to your daughter. That is fair enough.

First of all, our focus now is Mrs. Brown. Do your best to make her comfortable. Anytime she needs to see her doctor, take her to her appointment. Assist her with the use of her medications. Thank God money is not a problem. If there is any new medication in the market, talk about it with the doctor. Continue to do research and provide feedback to Mrs. Brown's doctor. Let's hope that the situation will not get worse. I am happy to know that you found a caregiver who Mrs. Brown is getting used to – even though it was hard at first. She calls the caregiver Jean, her own sister's name because she thinks the caregiver is her sister. Since Mrs. Brown had a good relationship with Jean, she should get along well with the caregiver. You mentioned that the caregiver works four hours daily. Her invaluable assistance should give you some time to rest and to do things on your own. Continue to trust her and let her be in charge any time she comes in.

In regards to Rob's fear of who is going to be the next patient, worrying cannot stop the disease. There are two things that I believe can prevent it: 1) Jane should be talking with her doctor to conduct tests to make early diagnosis and to discuss what can be done to prevent and/or delay the onset of the disease. 2) You need to increase your faith in God and believe that God is able to stop what people may call generational curse. That is why Jesus came to redeem us from the curse of the law. What we don't know can kill us. God's word says my people perish for lack of knowledge.

God is able to prevent it from happening to Jane and your daughter. As God told the Israelites that if they do what is right in his eyes and pay attention to his commands and keep his law, he says: "I will not bring on you any of the diseases I brought on the Egyptians, for I am the LORD, who heals you" (Exodus 15:26) (NIV). This promise that was made when the Israelites were in Egypt is still for us today. Psalm 91 goes in parallel with this, too. Read them and claim them. We are new Israelites. We are children of God. God is not only able to heal us (Psalm 103:3). Isaiah 53:5 prophesied about Jesus Christ that "by his wounds we are healed" (NIV). He is also able to cover us with the blood of Jesus Christ. Instead of getting worried, talk to God and he knows how to handle your present and future situations.

It is good you are spending more time with each other and that your frustrations are diminishing. Try to increase the time you have for each other and also the time you spend with God. Pray and meditate on the word of God. Exercise faith. God is good all the time. Pray for healing for Mrs. Brown and prevention for Jane and your daughter. Do not let Alzheimer's disease lord over you. Prevention is better than cure. May God listen to you while praying and be there for you all the time. God bless you.

Dear Jane & Rob,

I am delighted to know that Mrs. Brown and her caregiver are getting along great. The caregiver drives her everywhere. She even drove Mrs. Brown to the city of her birth and drove by her childhood home. Mrs. Brown seems to be happier and talking more. She likes praying with her caregiver and enjoys reciting Psalm 23. She plays the organ and enjoys singing old hymns. Good for her.

It is good news to know that you are getting along better. You were away for a weekend to see your grandchildren, which you have not been able to do for two or three years. Since Mrs. Brown's caregiver is doing great with Mrs. Brown, I will like to suggest that you find time to enjoy yourselves, try to be there for your children and grandchildren. It is not only Mrs. Brown that needs you, your children and their families also need you. If the two of you cannot be present at a function with your family at a time; you can take turns, and if an occasion is a must for both of you, try to find a solution to it. Try to be good to the caregiver so that you will be able to keep her for long. I am also happy to hear that you have been to your doctor to do tests and there was no cause for alarm (everything is negative). Great news!

I am hoping you will continue to have a restful retirement. However, you don't need to retire from praying and studying the Word of God. Communicate with him as much as you can. The more you communicate with God, the more you have peace inwardly and outwardly. Being at peace with God will promote peace in your marital life. Having peace in your life and marriage will eliminate frustration in your home. Alzheimer disease can be a kind of a vehicle driving you to God and reconstructing your marriage. Do not allow it to tear down your marriage but to build it up. God knows how to keep Mrs. Brown happy and comfortable. She is almost 90. I hope you will have a big birthday celebration for her.

There are many couples everywhere that are facing the same problems here and there. Some are caring for their parents who are cancer patients and other kind of diseases or illnesses. Some are not their parents, but their spouses, or brother/ sister or one of their children. Frustrations, fear, anger, stress and so on can be a by-product of life's trials. How can you be a good help to people in those categories? What about starting a support group in your area? You may take a particular disease or just general support group for immediate family member of caregivers. I believe you can do it. God is able to help hundreds of people who are frustrated with serving as caregivers for people with long term diseases, especially seniors like you who are caring for seniors. God is able to use you to bring healing to people who are hurting. Why not? You can do it, yes you can. May God bless you with all you may need to pass on peace and joy that Jesus Christ brought to the world. I promise you my prayer and support. Let me know if there's any way I can help.

Dear Rob & Jane,

It gives me pleasure to know that you are doing much better, you are happier and having fun together. And Mrs. Brown is also doing well. She was delighted to see many people come to her 90th birthday. Even though she was not fully aware of whose birthday it was. Thanks for sharing the information. You said she kept on asking whose birthday it was. However, if she is aware that there is a birthday celebration, it means she is not doing too badly. It may likely be painful for Jane sometimes, but you have to accept it as it is. People sometimes say that it can be worse. In all things, the apostle Paul says we should give thanks (1 Thess. 5: 18). We should thank God and wait and see what future holds for her.

I am also glad that you have started a "senior cares for senior support group"- that is wonderful! It is also nice to hear that you are getting help from your pastor and prayer meeting group. Are all the group members from your church? If yes, is it possible to make it known to people outside your church members? The advertisement can be through churches or by word of mouth. Think and pray about it. You also mentioned that you are thinking of starting another group for all ages. Caring for parents with long-term illnesses may even be more stressful for younger couples who are in the workforce and have younger children. They may find their caretaker role difficult and they will surely need a support group. Life may be so stressful or even depressing. However, if one knows that s/he can get some support, it will make life easier.

In fact, you may be surprised to see couples who have special needs children coming to the general support group. Many young couples are suffering in silence. They need people to love them, to hug them, and to tell them that they will be okay. Knowing that someone cares for you, and/or understands what you are going through and tries to encourage you is fantastic. You need to do your best to represent Christ in the lives of many people, couples or singles who are crying out for help day in day out and no one is there for them. Everyone seems to be too busy. People need you, but not withstanding, you have to take good care of yourselves, too. Do not over do anything. Don't allow burnout. Whenever you start a group or a branch, do not hesitate to delegate power to people who are capable of doing things in a godly way. Note; the Good News is not good news until it is shared.

It will be a good idea to learn from Jethro, Moses' Father-in-law. When Jethro knew how busy Moses was, he advised Moses to choose people to represent him to settle disputes among the Israelites. Jethro did not want his son-in-law to burn himself out (Ex. 18:1-27). I also don't want the two of you to wear yourselves out. Train people prayerfully and delegate responsibility to them. I will join you in prayer and if there is anything I can do to help out, do not feel shy to ask. Give me a ring or send me an email, I will do my best to help out. Do you mind if I pray with you?

Lord, we thank you for the many unpleasant things which come our way that you have turned into blessings for us and others. Thank you for what you have been doing for, and through, Rob and Jane. I pray that you will continue to uphold them, bless their family, and be with Mrs. Brown. Give them, oh Lord, all they need in the ministry of encouraging others. Grant peace, joy, and happiness to everyone Rob and Jane are coaching or ministering to, in Jesus' name.

Chapter 7
Dan & Rose – Marriage with Grief Encounter

Dear Dan & Rose,

Dan, I was so concerned when Rose shared your story with me. I believe Rose
has told you that I was going to write you. Your parents, Dan, had an accident
six months ago. Your mom died on the spot. Your dad was taken to the hospital
and stated to ask for his wife. When he heard that she had died, he started to cry
that he had killed his best friend, and a godly wife. He found it hard to embrace
the news and four days after the accident, he went into a coma and died within
two days. It is sad that this happened to godly people like your parents. Rose
made me to understand further that for the past five months you have been
out of control. You have not been yourself. You are angry, blame yourself, and
have given up or withdrawn from many things around the house, even from your
children. Rose, in her own case is frustrated and feels that there has been an
adverse effect on your marital life. You have stopped going to church. Initially,
Rose tried to go without you but she has stopped because she doesn't like to
continuously answer the question, "how and where is Dan?" She seems to be
tired of everything.

Dan and Rose, as I said before, I will like to express my condolences to both of you
and to Dan in particular. In a situation like this, it is difficult to know what to say.
Two things are important here, you, Dan, in particular are hurting, and your grief
seems to be so deep and unbearable. The second danger here is your marriage -
both of them go hand-in-hand. Grief in your home is causing problems in your
marriage. Let me talk about grief first. Dan you stopped going to church. To me, it
seems you are angry with God. Your parents were very active in their church. Your
dad was the chairperson of the church board, while your mom was the secretary
of the Ladies' Association. They used to go to prayer meetings and bible study
almost every week. Perhaps you are wondering, why God allowed that kind of
incident to happen. How come such a godly couple has to die like that. You never
thought that you would lose your parents in their 70s.

It is not always easy to know God's mind or plans for individuals. God's plans are
not ours. Your parents have done their best for you, your family, for God and their
church. Years ago, the Apostle Paul tried to comfort people like you who were so
sorrowful over the loss of their loved ones. He said: "Brothers, we do not want
you to be ignorant about those who fall asleep, or to grieve like the rest of man,
who have no hope. We believe that Jesus died and rose again and so we believe
that God will bring with Jesus those who have fallen asleep in him. According to
the Lord's own words, we tell you that we who are still alive, who are left till the
coming of the Lord, will certainly not precede those who have fallen asleep. ---
Therefore encourage each other with these words" (I Thess. 4:13-18) (NIV). Paul
was right. We should not be ignorant, your parents did not die; they are sleeping

in the Lord. Jesus himself said: "Do not let your hearts be troubled. Trust in God; trust also in me. In my Father's house are many rooms; if it were not so, I would have told you. I am going there to prepare a place for you" (John 14: 1-3) (NIV). God called your parents home when their rooms were ready. Trust that your parents are at rest. They are at peace. No sorrow or sickness for them. Let the joy of hope for eternal life replace sorrow and despair in your lives. May God comfort you. Keep in touch. I will write you again.

Dear Dan & Rose,

You are one-hundred per cent right. God indeed is our comfort. He is a present help in the time of trouble. He will not leave us fatherless or motherless. It is good to hear that you are gradually coming back to God. You have been back to praying together and even with your children.

You are absolutely right to say that your parents will be resurrected one day. In fact, that is our – all Christians' – hope. The resurrection of Jesus Christ enables us to know that when Jesus comes back those who died will be resurrected, together with those who are alive, we will meet him in the air. I Corinthians 15 tells us the story of the resurrection of Jesus; the resurrection of the dead in the Lord; and the resurrection of the body. To be honest with you, the apostle Paul was right. The empty tomb of Jesus Christ made us to believe that there is hope for our own resurrection. And if Christ has not been raised, our faith is futile and useless and our sins remain unforgiven. "Then those also who have fallen asleep in Christ are lost. If only for this life we have hope in Christ, we are to be pitied more than all men" (I Cor. 15: 17-19) (NIV).

So my brother and sister in the Lord, be cheerful, Mr. and Mrs. Johnson are with the Lord and will be raised from the dead one day. Even though you have been doing better emotionally and spiritually, I would like to encourage you to find yourselves a support group and go back to church. I do not know the role that your pastor and the church in general have played in the situation. Regardless what that is, even if they played little or no role in your recovery from grief, I will still suggest that you go back to church or you look for another church to attend. This is not only for you but also for your children, who should go back to Sunday school. It has been over a year that you have not been attending church. Think about it and pray about it as well.

It is okay to be angry with God sometimes, but we need to turn our anger to prayer. King David was very good at that. There are many communities and individuals' laments in the Psalms, but most of them, if not all, turned into prayers – prayer of thanksgiving or petitions. You can do the same, too. God understands. If the anger is still there, tell him to help you to get over your anger toward him, yourself or yourselves or anyone else. Pray to God to forgive you and to fully restore you back to himself. Your children need you. Do not be like the church in Sardis, it had a reputation of being alive, but guess what? It was dead (Rev. 3:1). As God said to that church, "Wake up! Strengthen what remains and that is about to die, for I have not found your deeds complete in the sight of my God" (Rev. 3:2) (NIV). God wants you to wake up and play your roles as a father to your children. Your parents have done their best with you. It is now your turn to do your best with your children. God did not kill your parents. Your wife and children or you are also not at fault. The good news is your parents are at peace and resting from all troubles and worldly problems. You and your family should celebrate their good lives and good memories. It will be appropriate for you and Rose to be back on your knees together. The devil is at work all the time. Don't give him any opportunities to set a trap for your marriage or family. Try to be wiser than him. God is able to restore you back to your roles at home and at church. Remove the garments of sadness, grief and sorrow away from you and put on the joy of Christ, his peace, love, and hope. The joy of the Lord is your strength (Neh. 8:10). "Be joyful always; pray continually; give thanks in all circumstances for this is God's will for you in Christ Jesus (I Thess. 5: 16-18) (NIV). God Bless you.

Dear Rose & Dan,

I'm happy the two of you have gone back to church and your children are happy to see their dad playing with them both inside and outside the home. Your pastor visited you and prayed with you. He invited you to a "grief share group" in your church. You seem to like it. In our conversation on the phone, I understood that Dan has quit drinking. He was trying to cover up his anger and grief with alcohol. Dan realized that alcohol could only help for a while and does not eliminate the problem. The real solution to the problem is to face it, deal with it and get healing through an appropriate way.

Though you are both doing well, you still need time to talk and Rose needs to express her disappointment that she was abandoned during the grief crisis. Dan, you need to apologize to Rose and to the children as well. It is also time to start communicating effectively and to renew your commitment to each other. Your children need to know and see that your marital health is back on track. Although your love for each other is not that worn out, it has been shaken and you have to reaffirm your love for each other. You promised each other unconditional love (agape) about ten years ago.

The grief wave should not stop your love or affect your relationship. Let the grief wave pass over you totally and come back in a strong way to rebuild your marital relationship. It is time for each one of you to start to care for each other and to try to take on a double role, as husband and "father" and as wife and "mother", especially since you have both lost your parents. I know the death of Dan's parents has brought back memories of Roses' parents whom she lost six years ago. She has been doing great. I am well pleased with that, not withstanding, parents are parents. Your children don't have any living grandparents. It must be hard on both of you as well as your children. But it is good to know that God is there for you as the all in all for your children. He has no grandchildren. Both you and your children can call him your Father. He will be a good Father to you all. Let the wave of grief pass and allow the wave of joy, peace and comfort to come to you.

I hope you will allow the word of God to dwell in you richly. Jesus Christ will not stop inviting you to come unto him with your heavy burdens, he has promised to give you rest (Matt. 11:28). Cast upon him your grief and sorrow, he cares for you so dearly (Ps. 55:22; I Peter 5:7). The couple that prays together stays together. Be one in all things. Care for each other. Don't allow grief to lord over you, instead, let it be under your feet. The Lord of peace will crush Satan (grief) under your feet shortly (Rom. 16:20). Keep fit in the Lord. God bless you always.

Dear Dan & Rose,

You are doing great. The getaway weekend you had two weeks ago, was a good idea. You said you attended a workshop on grief recovery last month, fantastic. Since you have been communicating better, having fun as you used to, and your prayer life is back to normal and even getting better than before, you should keep the ball rolling. Everything works for good for those who believe in God (Rom. 8:28).

The plan for a combined memorial service for your parents is a good idea. It will be a good lesson for your children who did not know much about their grandparents – maternal grandparents in particular. I will imagine that you will invite friends and relatives. The people who knew how your loss affected you - Dan in particular - have to see a different couple at the memorial service. They will be able to see some laughter, smiles, and joy in both of you. The service may likely be a form of thanksgiving for your family. Thanking God for the lives of your four parents! Their lives need to be celebrated with thanksgiving. Even though they were all 'dead' or asleep in the Lord in an untimely manner, their deeds are following them. The good things or acts God enabled them to do or perform need to be remembered, especially by all the grandchildren not only yours but of your brothers and sisters, too. I hope all your brothers and sisters will be able to come to your city and celebrate it together.

I will like to suggest that you take the avenue of the memorial service to tell your story to your brothers, sisters and friends. The story of healing from grief may likely start a process of healing for anyone who may be in your former shoes. The testimony should include how Dan started to cover up his anger and grief with alcohol and the consequent impact of the drinking on the marriage and home life. Dan's recovery and the other steps you have taken should also be shared. I hope your "Grief Share Group" will be invited to give you moral support.

Share with your pastor that the memorial service is not only a party, but also an opportunity to help those who may be hurting or overwhelmed by grief. Grief is not a friend of anyone as it can kill. Many people become alcoholics or drug abusers. Some people are also under a deep depression and end up with suicidal thoughts or commit suicide. I am sure God will help you to touch others through your testimony.

The pastor should be told about the context of your testimony so that he will be able to plan the service along with your goal or focus of your testimony. At any rate, find time to pray about it. I promise to join you in prayer for every soul that will be there, most especially people who have been touched by grief. I have been blessed to know you and I wish you and your family all the best. Keep in touch. God bless you always.

Chapter 8
Russell and Jo – Marriage with Abuses

Dear Russell & Jo,

Bob and Sarah told you about me and I am happy to tell you what I think you need to do to make your marriage vibrant again. As of now, Jo is half at home and half somewhere else. You can't seem to communicate with each other. You fight almost every day. It is as if your love for each other no longer exists. Your 11 year old son wants to go with Jo, while your 13 year old wants to stay with Russell. You have never been to a counselor because Jo doesn't want to talk about it. Your boys have been acting out. They're always afraid to go to school and their grades have dropped.

As I listened to both of you during our telephone conversation, I realized that Jo has made up her mind to leave home, even though Russell seems to be ready to talk and work things out. The issues you need to iron out are significant. I guess things can be okay with you again, if both of you are ready to talk and let go of some of your ego. Life, most of the time, is a matter of choices. Life seems like an opportunity cost. If both of you can agree to work things out, I believe that it is possible to get the ball rolling again, but it will take both of you to agree and fight against the enemies of marriage. It takes two people to fight and to settle it. If you want us to be talking about the issues surrounding your marital problems, I will be ready to help out. At the same time, I will like to advise you to have your boys in mind. It will not be a good idea to be fighting in front of them or talking bad about each other with the boys. The boys don't need to be victims of your arguments or fights. Let them choose on their own, who they will stay or go with.

Since it seems that you have run out of "wine" in your marriage, perhaps prayerfully you will like to do what Mary the mother of Jesus Christ did, when the groom ran out of wine at the wedding in Cana at Galilee. The presence of Jesus Christ at the wedding brought good news to the groom and the story has not been too old for more than 2,000 years (John 2:1-11). Many marriages are in trouble today because Christ is not in their home or in the marital life. I know you are Christians, but there is a possibility that you forgot to take Jesus with you on your marital journey. Mary and Joseph did the same, when they went to the temple (Luke 2: 41-52). On their way home, they thought Jesus was on the way with them and hanging out with his peer, but they were wrong. It took them three days before they realized that Jesus was not on the way home, instead Jesus was in the temple. I wonder if you knew that the joy and peace Jesus brought to the world was not there in your marriage. It is never too late to invite him or to re-invite him to help out. It is time to use your God's lifetime warranty in your marriage. The fights, angers, hurts and so on, will be taken away. Shame will be replaced with honor in your marital life. Christ will never say it is too late. Think about it, and pray for courage to tell your story to Jesus together or individually. He is able to help you. Let me know how I can help. God bless you.

Dear Russell & Jo,

It was nice to talk to you on the telephone the other day. Russell, I hope you will let Jo see this letter. In case Jo has moved, I will be writing her separately, if you can let me have her address.

Jo, I can understand where you are coming from. To you, it is over, even though Russell is of the opinion that there is still room for a second chance. If you think having a break will make both of you realize your mistakes, go for it. However, I will like you to make sure that you are doing the right thing. We do not need to do things for right's sake, but sometimes for our marriages' sake. Do not just focus on your rights, but also try to consider your marriage's rights. I am not trying to impose anything on you, but to make sure that you are doing the right thing *for your marriage*. Allow the Holy Spirit to lead you, because those who are led by the Holy Spirit are the children of God (Rom 8:14).

I am wondering if you will consider seeing a Christian counselor or to talk with your pastor about your marital issues. If you have not done so recently, you should try talking with your pastor and ask him to pray for you. If your own prayer life is not *strong* enough, you may try to correct it. Remember, the couple that prays together stays together. Prayer, most of the time is like crazy glue that can glue broken or almost broken things back together. If you want to ponder it, we will see how it is going to work for you, otherwise, pray for each other wherever you go or live. Your children need prayers, too. They deserve the best. God has good plans for them, and he needs you to make the plans materialize in their lives.

I will not mind to meet with you, if you are willing. As people say, face to face is better than a hundred letters, emails or telephone calls. Think about it, if Jo is still interested in a second chance, I will find time to meet with you. Let me know what you want. Do whatever you can to save your marriage. God knows the best. He has a good plan for you and your children. Don't go outside God's will for you. Sixteen years ago, you exchanged your vows, you promised each other for better or for worse, you will love each other and not otherwise. We change, our plans or attitude are always subject to change. However, God never changes. His yes remains yes. He is the same yesterday, today and he will be the same forever (Heb. 13:8). When our yes changes to no, God understands, he does not only believe in second chances, but in many chances. I am here to help you choose rightly. Wrong choices may not only affect our today, it may affect our future and even our children and grandchildren's future, too. Allow God to tell you what to do and both of you have to humble yourselves to listen to him and follow his directions. Let me know what is going on and I will do whatever I can to be there for you. Bob and Sarah know that I don't give up on people. I always like to see that the end is not regrettable, but joyous. May God bless you always. Give my love to the boys.

Dear Russell,

Thanks for letting me know that Jo left home last week. How are you making out? Your 11-year-old Tim went with his mom, and your 13-year-old Sam stayed with you. How are you feeling about the whole situation? You mentioned on the phone that you should have done things better. Are you blaming yourself for the whole situation? How is Sam making out? He must miss his mom and brother.

First of all, I would like to advise you not to express your anger or frustrations in front of Sam. Don't make him a scapegoat or talk badly about his mom to him. Whatever is happening to both of you at home, I will like you to take it easy and demonstrate maturity to your boy. Whatever you say or do to the boys today will become history tomorrow. I will like to advise that both of you – you and Jo – make arrangements for the boys to see each other on a regular basis. They need to be talking and having fun together.

You said Jo wants to have full custody of both kids. She wants to fight and she is also asking too much for settlement. Could that be one of the reasons why you are angry? Most moms normally ask for full custody because they believe they are the best parent to care for their children, and young kids are sometimes more comfortable with their mothers. I am not trying to say that Jo should keep the boys. By the way, have you and Jo considered talking with a mediator to help you settle things? You do not need to fight - it takes two people to fight. It would be great, if you could suggest to Jo that both of you should be talking with a mediator.

All people concerned in most divorces are losers. The children are the biggest losers. The only ones who tend to gain in divorce proceedings are the lawyers. And you should be careful with the lawyers; many of them can be too pushy. Well, I can't blame them for making lots of money. They are doing their jobs. Do not spend a lot of money, if you don't need to. Try to be friends, find time to talk and try to be accommodating. If Jo is not ready to talk, do not be angry or worry, things will cool down later. And at the same time, you, too, should not try to initiate a fight. The more you fight, the more bitterness or anger will grow. There will be less bitterness and anger, if you can take it easy with each other. Talk and do not fight.

I will write Jo almost the same thing I am sending you. She sent me her address before she left home. She did not tell me when she would be leaving home. I am wondering if you've called her to tell her that you love her. If not, why not? But do not over-do it. At the same time, let her know that you miss her and Tim. Do you and Sam call Tim to say hi to him? Let Tim know that you love him, too. And Sam and Tim should be talking; they don't need to feel as if they are two families. It's good that Tim and his mom are not too far away from you. If possible, the boys should have fun together every weekend. Let me know how things are going with you. God bless you.

Dear Jo,

Thank you for giving me your address. Russell told me that you and Tim have moved out of the house. How are you making out? Do you like your new place? Does Tim like the area? Is he going to change school? I wish him all the best.

You've said over and over again that your marriage is over! Are you still of the same opinion? Or are you just taking a break to learn from your mistakes so that you can start over again? I suppose you are not taking a break because Russell told me that you want Sam as well and you plan to fight for him even in court. I agree with you that the boys should not be separated from each other. It is one hundred per cent true. The same principle is also applicable to you and Russell. What God has joined together nothing is supposed to separate it. God made a suitable companion (woman) for Adam, to hold hands and to do things together. Both husband and wife are supposed to be of the same flesh and bones (Gen. 2:20-24).

If it is true that you are ready to fight for everything, I will like to suggest that you try to take it easy. Perhaps you need to work on forgiveness. Until you forgive Russell, your mind will like to revenge and the more you think about verbal and emotional abuse you have received from Russell, the more anger and bitterness will be springing up in you. You don't need to keep malice in your mind. Too much anger is not good for you. Your liver doesn't need any poison and that is what too much anger may do to your liver. You will need to pray to God to help you forgive Russell.

By the way, when you move toward the path of forgiveness, you're doing yourself a big favor. God is able to help you to let go and let him. Jesus forgave his enemies and taught us to do the same. I sense that it must be hard on you, more so that he verbally abused you in front of your boys and he did not apologize right away. As Russell mentioned, you are ready to fight to have both boys and also for a better settlement. I suggested to him that the two of you should consider seeing a mediator so that you can save money.

You need to remember that the more you fight, the more the boys will be affected. Find a way to talk and to agree on many things by yourselves, however, before a meaningful discussion can take place, you have to communicate about your past. Both of you need to let go of egoism. Not just for the sake of your marriage or your children, but for your own sake.

As I've said to Russell, I will not mind to talk with you face to face, even though I am four hours away from you. Or you can find a Christian counselor who will be able to lead you to deal with your grievances and help you to let go of the offences. Think about it. Try to be having friendly conversations with Russell any time you have to communicate.

How is your job going? Russell told me that you have been promoted to a managerial position. Congratulations. It's good to have good news during unpleasant situations. The good news is; God is there for us in any situation we find ourselves. I hope you will keep in touch with me. God bless you.

Dear Russell,

Greetings. I got your note. I understand that you have tried to reconcile with Jo. You made attempts to invite her to your house or to go to hers, but all your efforts have been futile. Jo told you that she is no longer interested in talking with you and that she has given up.

In fact, your case now is not about reconciliation, but to ask for forgiveness. Jo told me that you verbally and emotionally abused her many times. As such, you need to seek forgiveness from Jo. However, I cannot promise you on behalf of Jo that everything is going to be alright as a result. But if I were you, I would take a route of repentance and seek pardon from her. There are different ways of doing it. One of the ways, since she is not ready to come to you or allow you to go to her, is to write her a letter to let her know that you have realized your mistakes and you will like her to forgive you. You can also promise her that you will treat her with respect, and that you will not repeat such foolish actions again. Another step you may consider is to talk to one of her married best friends that you can trust to help you talk to her on your behalf or to facilitate your talk in her house. Whatever avenue you choose is fine, as long as you stop bugging her about reconciliation.

You also need to seek forgiveness from God and ask him to help you to deal with the situation. You should also seek anger management counseling. I wonder what causes your anger and what you have done about it in the past. Your children have seen you verbally abuse their mom. What kind of example have you been given to them? Perhaps the first step you need to take is to manage your anger and then apologize to Jo. The apology may likely be followed by reconciliation. When Jo sees that you have changed and become a new person, she will have to decide by herself, if she wants to go on a reconciliation route. Taking the time to talk with your children about your mistake and your bad behavior should be included in the process of forgiveness and reconciliation.

You should try to ask God to forgive you and teach you how to use your tongue. You need to control your anger and tongue. James the apostle writes in James 3:3-12 (NIV) that the tongue can become a wild fire, if not properly channeled, can destroy relationships, family and friendships. Please read the passage over and over again and prayerfully do something about it. You cannot do it on your own, but God is able and more than ready to help you to act accordingly. I believe if God wants you together again, he knows what to do and how to talk to Jo. If you want me to talk more about anger management or you want to find a counselor over there, please let me know. God loves you and I do. God bless you.

Dear Jo,

How are you making out? How is Tim doing? Thank you for your comments regarding my last letter and our telephone conversation.

I spoke to Russell and wrote him a letter. Are you still talking other than fighting about the boys and the settlement? You said that the separation is now official. Are you still angry at Russell? I can't blame you for being so, if you are. But I will like you to try to take it easy. God forgives us and he wants us to forgive those who sin against us. When Jesus Christ taught his disciples the Lord's Prayer, he asked them to say "Give us our food for today, and forgive us our sins, just as we have forgiven those who have sinned against us ---"(Matt 6:11-12) (NLT). Jesus went on to say "If you forgive those who sin again you, your heavenly Father will forgive you. But if you refuse to forgive others, your Father will not forgive your sins" (Matt 6:14-15) (NLT).

Jesus wants us to forgive others, if we want to receive forgiveness from God. Jesus wanted his disciples to know more about forgiveness. He instructed them in Matthew 18: 28-35. Peter, like many people, wanted to know how often we should forgive before we can stop forgiving. Jesus replied "seventy times seven" (Matt 18:22). I am not sure, if Russell sinned against you that much in a day when you were living together.

I am not trying to impose anything on you. I just want to help you cope with your day to day life without being cranky. Pray to God to help you let go. I am not talking about reconciliation yet, but the betterment of your life. Both of you need to forgive each other. Russell said he used to be offended in regards to your spending habits. He said that in spite of your good income, you were always in the red. Management of finances is what Russell said is one of the biggest marital problems you had. However, that does not justify his abuse toward you. Russell needs anger management, while you need financial management. Perhaps since both of you lacked one kind of management maybe that translates to your lack of marital management. This is not the time to blame yourself because of one reason or another, but time for healing and adjustment. You need two things to prayerfully work on - forgiveness and financial management. If you need any help in any of them, please, feel free to contact me.

You said that you and Russell have been to the mediator but there was no agreement. The case of separation, settlement and custody of both boys are in the hands of your lawyers. You admitted that it is very expensive, but you thought you don't have any other choice than taking that road. I don't want to judge you, but at the same time, you had many other choices, but you have chosen that route. It's okay. Just make sure that you are doing things according to the leadership of the Holy Spirit. Do not let the situation drag you away from God, but toward God. He is a God of many chances. He wants us to repent and turn away from our wrong ways. If we do, he is more than willing to restore us back to himself without any gap between him and us. All the best, as you are pondering on what the next step in your life will be. God bless you. Keep in touch.

Dear Russell,

How are things with you and Sam? You must be disappointed that Jo divorced you after all the efforts you have put into improving your relationship – that is, the anger management workshops you attended, the adjustment you have made with your attitude toward her and life in general. You wrote Jo letters of apologies, you prayed a lot and your friends and church also joined you in prayers that things will get better and be resolved. How are you feeling that your efforts were fruitless? How is Sam handling the situation? What about Tim?

Well, I believe you have done your best. Things did not work out as you would have liked. It seems as if it is over. It must feel like the death of a family member, especially to Sam and Tim. I hope they are not too upset. I believe you should never say "never" When there is life, there is hope. Do not lose hope. Don't allow discouragement to prevent you from praying for her and for the will of God for both of you. It is not time to be angry with her or yourself, even at God. If God wants you back together, he knows what to do. Continue to do what you have been doing. Don't lose hope, try to be cool, you shouldn't allow anger to surface again. Backward never, forward ever. Pray for her and also for the boys. She seems to be cooling down with regards to full custody of both boys. But according to our last conversation, she is still fighting about the house. I am wondering why both of you are so interested in the house. Perhaps to give room for peace, you can sell the house and share the money.

But if there is any significance to the house, that will be a different story. However, if there is no importance, you need to find a solution to the issue, since it is more or less a bone of contention between you. Do not focus on what can divide you but on what will unify you.

Sam and Tim should not be scapegoats of your divorce plight. They need to see each other as brothers. Although they are living separately, they can still be brothers, and should visit each other on a weekly basis. Both of you should make your boys a top priority by looking after their welfare. They deserve the best. They should be one family and not two. You need to stand by your goal to be a better person and to get rid of your anger. Being a new person will be beneficial to you, your family and others. Unless she says no to you, don't close the door of any opportunities. Call her and talk to her with respect not with anger or feeling of being rejected or with a disappointed tone. If she still has a small room inside of her to reconcile with you, she may likely be testing you to see if it will be a good idea for her to be open to something like that.

I will not be surprised to see people trying to advise you positively and otherwise. You have to be selective about people you seek advice from. There are some so called friends who would like you to be like them and try to coach you on how to fight. Some ladies who are interested in you will consider it awkward to know that you are waiting to see if Jo will change her mind. All I am saying is, be-careful. Talk to good friends and to Jesus the best Friend who will never mislead anyone. God bless you.

Dear Jo,

How is life treating you now? You have gotten what you have been talking about. How does that make you feel? Are you happier now than before? How is Tim? He will be 13 soon. Does he miss his father? How is he treating you as a teenager?

I am glad to hear that you and Tim went for dinner at Russell and Sam's house- that was nice of you. The children need to see a sense of family in all of you, even though you are divorced but you and Russell are still their parents, regardless of the situation. Let them continue to see a sense of belonging. The boys should be doing stuff together, maybe on weekends. They should not see a trace of disagreement or fight in you. You can make a difference. Many divorced couples do fight, but you don't have to be like them. Let other divorcees see Christ in you. Non-Christian divorcees may advice you according to a worldly philosophy, but you have to behave as an ambassador of Jesus in the circumstances you find yourself. We need to handle things differently from other people outside Christendom. By the way, is there any support group around you? A group like "Divorce Care" will be good for you. The situation you are in now is not the matter of asking God "why?", but "what?" Many people express bitterness toward God, asking him why he allowed divorce in their marriages. It will be wise for you to be asking God what he wants you to learn and what he wants to achieve from this ugly situation. Something good can come out of this circumstance. Remember you are not alone. Thousands of couples have seen the death of their marital lives. It will be a wise choice to safe yours.

I believe I asked you when we were talking on the phone, if there is someone in your life, your answer was no. As of now, I will encourage you to take it easy before you take any step in that direction. You need to pray hard and to be sure. The rate of divorce in second marriages is higher than first marriage, so Jo, "be sure." By the way, have you closed your mind totally to any possibility of being together again with Russell? I know it's too early to be thinking that way. But you have to be open to the Holy Spirit, and try to take it easy.

The most important thing now for both you and Russell is to be friends, not just for your boys, but also for your health. Don't give room to anger. Don't let the devil continue to remind you of the past. Close the chapter you have read and open a new chapter. Forgiveness on your own part is very necessary. Let go and let God. I've said this before. I hope you will not mind me repeating myself. May the God of peace grant you peace all the time. You need good Christian friends who you'll be able to talk with. Are you still going to the same Church? If yes, how does that make you feel – you and Tim sitting on a different pew from Russell and Sam?

Above all, make your request known to God; do not hesitate to pray for your teenage boys. Ask God to help them out in their undertakings. I don't think it is easy nowadays to be a teenager as well as a single parent but you will never be alone. God said, "Never will I leave you; never will I forsake you" (Heb. 13:5) (NIV). I will be praying for you as usual. Don't be deceived, God loves you and he cares, and I do. God bless you always.

Dear Russell,

Greetings to you in the wonderful name of Jesus. How are you making out? I understand better now with regards to the house. You used the money your paternal grandfather willed you to buy the house. I am glad that Jo agreed with you to keep the house and settle with her. She has gotten her own share of the house. Good. Things seem to be getting better. You and Sam went to celebrate Sam's birthday at Jo's and she and Tim came over for your birthday. You said she has been calling you more often than before. And you have been behaving yourself. Good stuff.

So what is going on in your mind? What have you been talking about lately? Do you think she is willing or open to reconciliation? One of you has to be bold enough to introduce the subject. What do you think? At least that is what you have been waiting and praying for. If you are convinced that you are both ready, I *will* pray to God to give you boldness and wisdom to start the discussions. This case, to me, is just like dating for the first time! Can you remember how you started your friendship at the university where you met? You need to start by improving your friendship. Sending her notes, flowers, and telling her that you love her. Let her know that she is very beautiful and that you love her unconditionally. You don't have to say what is in your mind yet, don't rush. Be smart. After a few weeks of seeing each other steadily and knowing for sure that she is more than ready, then you may propose to her. Don't forget she is a "free agent" now. You have to start all over. She is not your wife legally, but your ex.

When you express your desire to her and she says yes to you, I will recommend that you find time to pray and read the bible together. Fights, misunderstandings, or problems will be more serious or more damaging to both of you as well as your boys. After you have agreed together, I will suggest that you go and tell your pastor, more so that Jo still comes to your church, even though you said she and Tim sat with you and Sam on the same pew last Sunday. The pastor should not be told by someone else, but by you.

I wonder if Sam and Tim know what is going on. As time goes on, you will need to tell them. I will guess that they will be delighted. To children, divorce of parents seems like a death of the family. And the coming together of the parents will be like a resurrection of the family. Remember, the story of the resurrection of Jesus Christ was just like a joke to many Jews, even to some of the disciples, it was a fable. The boys may likely be over joyous. Ask them to join you in prayer. They are no longer kids, they are growing up. Sam will soon graduate from high school.

Let me know how things are going. If there is anything I can do, I will be more than willing to help out. It is a big step that needs more patience, faith, love and above all, more payers. I will be praying for you. Let me say a short prayer now:

Our Lord God, you are the author of marriage, we thank you for Jo and Russell; for the past five years of separation you have been there for them. Russell needs your wisdom to approach Jo about reconciliation. Work things out by yourself and by your power. Let your will be done in their lives, oh Lord. Give both of them understanding of your mind and plans for their lives. Speak to both of them in the language they will understand. In Jesus' name we have prayed. Amen

Dear Jo,

Greetings to you, Jo. I was delighted to hear that you and Russell have begun talking seriously and that he has proposed to you again to marry you and that you have said yes. Amazingly, he has given you an engagement ring. Wow!! I am happy for both of you.

If you will not mind, I will like to share this letter with him, and from now on, I will be writing you together like before. Although, you are not living together and you are not Mr. & Mrs. yet, I will still prefer to write you together, it will save me time and stop me from repeating myself. If both of you have any problems with that; let me know. You said you have been seeing each other every weekend and a couple of days during the week.

I will like to suggest to you to find time to talk about why your first marriage collapsed and how you can prevent it in your upcoming wedding. If I can remind you what I know, Russell used to abuse you verbally and emotionally. Anger was the cause of Russell's impatient actions. His argument was that your spending was out of control. You need to find lasting solutions to the problems. What I will suggest is that you deal with one problem at a time. Questions that need to be asked would be why and what? the problem of anger or abuse for example. Why did Russell get angry? What can you do to prevent Russell from being angry? You don't need to be in a rush. If you rush into your marriage, there is possibility that you will rush out again. It will be more painful. So you have to be very careful.

Don't be deceived that it is not right to get back together as husband and wife after divorce. Some people hold the opinion that when you say good night somewhere, you are not supposed to say good evening any longer. This idea or opinion is not applicable to you. The house of Israel would have perhaps gone back to Egypt when they were on the way to the promise land had the Red Sea remained passable. Their faith was not what sustained them, but circumstances. Your faith, your courage and God himself will enable you to stand tall with regard to your decision. God will sustain you and lead you to the right steps to be taken. Taking time to pray and study the word of God together will be very essential. I will recommend you to be reading (I Cor. 13; Eph. 5: 22-33; I Pet. 3:1-7; Prov. 31) and any other passages in the bible that may speak to you personally on other matters. Don't underrate the power of prayer. It takes God's grace for two persons to agree, and two are better than one (Amos 3:3). Be on your knees together, let God know what you want and what is better for you and your boys. A prayer less couple is a powerless couple, more prayer means more power and joy; less prayer means less power, less joy, lack of harmony and more problems.

Commit your ways, your tomorrow, and your marriage to the Lord and he will sustain you: "commit your way to the Lord, trust in him and he will do this: he will make your righteousness shine like the dawn, the justice of your cause like the noonday sun" (Ps. 37:5-6) (NIV). As I've promised you before, I will be there for you.

Dear Russell & Jo,

So Jo has two engagement rings. I hope the previous one is still there somewhere. Congratulations to both of you on your engagement. The wedding is coming up. You have four months to prepare for it. I will not be surprised if people call you and ask you how you manage to end up in marriage after divorce for about three years. I hope you will be able to share your stories with them. It is not totally over until it is over.

I will like to talk to you more on how you can save your marriage from unnecessary disputes.

Communication is one of the *clues* to the success of your marriage. I will like to encourage you to plan for how to have meaningful and effective communication in your marriage. You don't need to give room for arguments but for better understanding of each other. When you cannot understand what your partner is saying, that is not communication. It is a waste of time. Another killer of communication you need to avoid is assumption. Don't assume that your partner understands what you are trying to say, that is not communication. Ambiguous words are other aspects of communication you do not need in your talk. Speak simple language, not big terminology or big words or a confusing analogy. Speak loud and clear. The receiver of communication should not hesitate to ask questions for clarity. It is better that way than to assume wrongly what the speaker is saying. Don't speak or conclude for the speaker, let him/her conclude for him/herself. Share your joys, burdens, concerns, feelings, hurts and so on.

Another aspect you need to iron out before you say "I do" is your budget. It will be appropriate for you, in my opinion, to talk first before you spend money. We must learn from our past mistakes. It is good that Jo has undergone a workshop on how to manage your resources. God has blessed us and put us in charge of our finances. We should try to be good stewards. We are accountable for how we manage our resources. Proverbs 31 will be a good chapter to read, particularly verses 10-31 which describe the wife of a noble character. This noble wife in character knew what to buy and where to buy them. Before you spend any big amount of money, you need to agree on it. God wants us to be wise and not to be slaves to credit cards with high interest rates. You must buy what you need and not what you want at a particular time. You need to know how to do your shopping, look for sales when necessary. Above all, do not overlook what you can talk about. Effective communication will save you a lot of time in fighting or arguing. Use it well and your marital joy will never suffer. Also your marital life will never be disoriented. Keep in touch. Be blessed in the Lord.

Dear Russell & Jo,

I am happy for you that you are moving forward with your wedding plans as well as with changing things around for better. Sam and Tim are looking forward to seeing the day of the wedding. It's going to be a big turn-around event. You have met twice with the pastor who will be performing the wedding and the sessions were good. I am glad to hear that, too.

As I promised when we were talking on the phone the other day, I am writing you another letter about commitment and love. I believe you started your previous marital life very well and your love for each other was sincere, too. Down the road, the events or unforeseen circumstances affected your vows of commitment and love for each other. As you're about to enter into an old but new relationship, I will encourage you to start over again, as you did for dating, engagement, etc. You will be making a new covenant which I believe God is going to help you keep until death do you part. Before you separated and after your separation and divorce you were still committed to your jobs. Because you were doing well at work both of you continued to get promotions upon promotions. You love your jobs and because of that, your bosses love you and you received benefits or rewards for your hard work. The efforts you put in at your work places paid off for you. If you can put in similar efforts to keep your vows in marriage, you will receive many rewards day in day out. Your rewards will include joy, peace, happiness, satisfaction, harmony, oneness, etc. I hope you will do your best to keep your commitment intact and to increase your love for each other every day.

Since you have separated until you started to date again – perhaps when you say "I do" you will realize the benefits of being together. Two are always better than one. Two hands will wash each other better than what only one can. The author of Ecclesiastics says: "Two are better than one, because they have a good return for their work: if one falls down, his friend can help him up. But pity the man who falls and has no one to help him up! Also, if two lie down together, they will keep warm. But how can one keep warm alone? Though one may be overpowered, two can defend themselves. A cord of three strands is not quickly broken" (Eccl. 4:9-12) (NIV).

You need determination to stand by each other to uphold each other, to keep each other warm, and be there for each other. Do not take commitment and love lightly; they are very essential tools you need to keep your marriage alive. The fall of a person is not the end of his/her life. If a person falls and stays on the ground or floor, s/he may be there forever. One needs some encouragement to stand up and keep going. That is what you are doing. Keep going and don't look back. God will enable you to stand tall in the new relationship you are entering.

Continue to pray for a successful wedding day, but remember a wedding lasts for only a day while a marriage is supposed to last forever. God is able to help you to build a new solid home on the rock. I will join others to be praying for you before and after your wedding day. Keep hope alive.

Dear Jo & Russell,

Greetings. I am well pleased to hear that your wedding went well. The service and reception were great. Your parents from both sides were there as well as your brothers and sisters. It must have been a good reunion for all of your family members. You were away on your honeymoon for a week. Fantastic! Welcome back!

How does coming together again make you feel? Your love for each other has been renewed. The new commandment, to use Jesus Christ's phrase, "love each other," (John 15:17) (NIV) must be given you a good feeling. The vows you exchanged were like the old ones, but technically they are new. I hope you will do your best to keep them forever. What God has joined together we should not allow anything to separate it.

I told you that I will be writing you about adjustment. You both have lived separately for about five years. I am wondering how hard it was on you. I believe you will not like the situation to repeat itself. In order not to experience the lonely life again, be cautious of the similar problems that led to your divorce. Both of you admitted that you need a change. Without adjustment, a change may not likely be possible. First of all, you've lived independent lives for some years now. You didn't need to talk to anyone before you make your own decisions. That needs to change now. Spending money, travelling and even going home late from work need adjustments. In the early years of your acquaintances with each other – during your first dating and couple of your first years of marriage – you made some adjustments. You will need to allow history to repeat itself. Whatever you enjoy doing and you know will hurt your partner, you should be careful about it. Paul the apostle tried to address something similar to adjustment and warned the Corinthian church members not to make others who are not so strong in faith fall because of what they are doing or eating. He argues: "Be careful, however, that the exercise of your freedom does not become a stumbling block to the weak. For if anyone with a weak conscience sees you have this knowledge eating in an idol's temple, won't he be emboldened to eat what has been sacrificed to idols? So this weak brother, for whom Christ died, is destroyed by your knowledge, when you sin against your brothers in this way and wound their weak conscience, you sin against Christ. Therefore, if what I eat causes my brother to fall into sin, I will never eat meat again so that I will not cause him to fall" (I Cor. 8: 9-13) (NIV).

The apostle Paul was smart, whatever will make your wife/husband angry or hurt, don't do it. Discipline goes with adjustment. You have to discipline yourself for the sake of your partner and for the betterment of your marriage. You have to choose between your "right" and your marriage. Why is a big sacrifice highly necessary and how can you deny yourselves because of your marriage? Well, I believe it pays off. The agony of separation or divorce is unbearable, I guess. You have been there. I hope you will do whatever you can to prevent such pains of divorce from recurring. Do not see adjustment or discipline as stupid things to do to make your marriage survive. God loves you. Christ made a big sacrifice for us on the cross. He disciplined himself to undergo the agony and do you know what? It paid off for him and for us. We Christians are beneficiaries of his sacrifice on the cross, your children and their children would benefit from sacrifices you will be making for your marriage to survive. God bless you.

Dear Russell & Jo,

You're most welcome. I am glad I can help out in any little way, thank you for your note. I am happy to know that you are doing great and that your boys are happy. Sam's girlfriend visited you recently. You said she seemed to be a nice young lady. It is nice to hear that.

Sam must be happy to see you in love and together again. If he has been going out with the lady for almost two years without bringing her over to you, why now? This is to suggest to me that he is very proud of you and perhaps very pleased with the step of reconciliation that you have taken. Our children always look for good role models and Sam has found that in you now. You must be pleased that God enabled you to agree together to fall in love again. The step of forgiveness that both of you have taken will surely be beneficial not only to you and your marriage, but also to your boys and friends around you. Keep up the good job.

You had mentioned that you wanted me to talk a little bit about sexuality. You said you really enjoyed your sexual life for the first five years of your marriage. But after Tim was born, things went downhill. Although you are getting older, this is another honeymoon and another new beginning. This time your enjoyment of sexuality should not be limited to five years or so. You should allow yourselves to enjoy the special gift of God to married couples. Ask God for strength and courage to satisfy each other in the process of enjoying yourselves. When God said it is not good for a man to be alone that he would make a help mate for him, God wants couples to help and meet each other's needs, emotionally, physically and sexually.

Sexual intercourse is part of communication. During the exercise, the couple is engaged in non-verbal communication. If both sides are satisfied, it means they have an effective communication. Otherwise, it is the opposite. Do not just have sex for sex sake, make sure both of you enjoy yourselves, I believe you know what I mean. If the orgasm is not there, the sexual communication is not truly meaningful. You must appreciate your bodies and touching your bodies and giving thanks to God for giving you your beautiful wife and your handsome husband.

You must not wait until you are in bed or getting ready for bed to enjoy each other sexually. Admire each other in any way you can as time goes on before you are in bed. As God loves you, he wants you to love each other and to express it in different ways. You need to verbalize your love for each other as well as listen to and care for each other. When sexual love is not there, other aspects of love are incomplete. Do yourself a favor and express your love sexually. As you are trying to enjoy it, you must be appreciative to God. Some Christian couples pray before and after the sexual intercourse. The prayer being offered afterward is to thank and appreciate God for the gift of sexuality. If you have not been doing so, you may consider it. God desires our appreciations and I will imagine that he will be pleased, if we can thank him for the little and big things. Above all, let a genuine love rule your hearts. Hebrews 13:1 says "keep on loving each other as brother/ sister." I will say keep on loving each other as husband and wife. Christ loves us and the new commandment he gave us is to love each other. Agape love covers all multitudes of sins Show love to each other anywhere, in bed, living room, inside or outside. God loves you.

Dear Russell & Jo,

How are you making out? It is my joy to know that you are doing great. Your communication has improved, and both of you are adjusting very positively. Your sex drive is very good and you have been enjoying each other sexually. It's always great to hear good news.

Jesus Christ once said apart from him, we can do nothing. He says it well: "Remain in me, and I will remain in you, no branch can bear fruit by itself; it must remain in the vine. Neither can you bear fruit unless you remain in me. I am the vine; you are the branches. If a man remains in me and I in him, he will bear much fruit; apart from me you can do nothing. If one does not remain in me, he is like a branch that is thrown away into the fire and burned" (John 15:4-6) (NIV).

Many marriages have died because the couples did not see the necessity of allowing Jesus Christ in their marital lives. If Christ can be in the center of any marriage, it will make a big difference. At this juncture, I will like to advise you to allow Jesus Christ to be an unseen guest in your home all the time. If he is in your marriage, you will be able to tell him if there are any problems, he has all the tools to fix all or any problems you can imagine in your home. The lifetime warranty provided by God is yours. Use it in your marriage. Jesus himself sent out an invitation to all who are under the pressure of heavy burden, he promised to give them rest (Matt. 11:28).

I will suggest to you to give Jesus Christ a complete chance to rule or teach you how to cope with any or all marital difficulties. Call on him often, and don't wait until problem comes before you call unto him. Be on offensive not defensive. You need to know what Jesus wants and his mind. How? You can know his mind by studying his words and meditating on who he was, who he is and how he can transform ugly situation. You will need to study the bible and pray together, if possible to start your day with reading the words of God, praying and also to end it with bible reading, meditation and prayer. If you can read the bible and pray together in the morning, you will not end the day with an argument or a fight.

To stay together is to pray together, I like it other way around; to pray together is to stay together. God who institutionalized marriage wanted the marital couple to be one. "For this reason a man will leave his father and mother and be united to his wife, and they will become one flesh" (Gen. 2: 24) (NIV). The kind of oneness God wants from you is that you to be in him and he in you, it is important to stay connected with him through prayer and reading of his word. Any branch that is not on the main tree will be cut off, and what happens next? It dries up, and then thrown into the fire (John 15:6). Any marriage, Christian marriage in particular, that does not remain in Christ will or may dry up and end up in divorce or separation. It is a bitter experience. I believe you will not like to go through it again. To avoid it is to dwell in the Lord and to let his word richly dwell in you (Col. 3:16). Don't forget, apart from God you can do nothing.

It will also be good for you, if you can find a marriage support group or any marriage enrichment group that you can join or a workshop you can attend. Prevention is better than cure. God loves you and he wants the best for you. Give him a full authority to come and live in your home. May he continue to bless you.

Dear Russell & Jo,

I like your idea of not making a big deal of your first anniversary. To show people that second marriage with the same husband and wife can work you defer the celebration of your anniversary to the 3rd year. I was pleased to hear that it was a great celebration. Many people from your community, your workplaces and your friends from church and elsewhere were partakers of your celebration. You were able to share your story – what brought you together at your first wedding, how it dissolved and how you started all over again. I was indeed moved that you made people know that it is possible to "do it again." You made new from old. Good job.

As of now, I believe you will know that many eyes are on you, the devil will be more active to fight you and to make you swallow your testimony. Forward ever and backward never. He who has begun a good work in you will surely complete it (Phil. 1:6). God is able. He has helped you so far for the past three years. He will not leave you or forsake you (Heb. 13:5). As God instructed Joshua when he took Moses' position of leadership that the book of the law should not depart from his mouth, he is ordering you to stay in his word. God puts it this way to Joshua: "Be strong and very courageous. Be careful to obey all the law my servant Moses gave you; do not turn from it to the right or to the left, that you may be successful wherever you go. Do not let this Book of the law depart from your mouth; mediate on it day and night, so that you may be careful to do everything written in it. Then you will be prosperous and successful. Have I not commanded you? Be strong and courageous. Do not be terrified; do not be discouraged, for he is the Lord your God and will be with you wherever you go" (Josh 1:7-9) (NIV).

I will say Amen to that. Whatever you do or wherever you go, the presence of God will be with you, just continue to do whatever he tells you to do. I will also like to encourage you to refrain from referring to past hurts. Unless you want to laugh over your past, do not attempt to refer to them regardless how angry you are at each other. The past is behind you, you have learned from your mistakes. When you refer to past hurts, the devil would be happy and would try to make the past seem present. He may likely try to bring back your old nature – anger and bitterness – and to make a big deal out of it. The only time you can refer to the old days, however, would be for thanksgiving. After whatever discussions you have about it, end up thanking God that you are living in the present not in the past. Forgiveness took place years ago. You both need to be like your heavenly Father who says:

"Come now, let us reason together," says the Lord. Though your sins are like scarlet, they shall be as white as snow; though they are red as crimson, they shall be like wool" (Isa. 1:18) (NIV). When God forgives, he does without any reference to the past. Let it be in your marital life and teach others including your boys.

I am so blessed to know you. You have put more bliss to my counseling experiences. I hope you will not mind, if I refer to your story whenever I meet couples like you, who may likely want to come together or who may hesitate to reunite after their divorce. May God bless you and continue to uphold your marriage and bless many couples through you. It was Nice to know you.

Chapter 9
Ed and Ruby – Marriage and Jealousy

Dear Ed & Ruby

It was nice chatting on the phone with you the other day. I will like to congratulate Ruby on her PhD degree. Wow! Ed, you also have made it to the top. You now have two PhD degrees in your household. Ed got his four years ago. Ruby you started when Ed put an end to his. Good job on your Academic achievements. Ed, you have not been able to get a full time position as a professor, but Ruby was able to secure one in her department. She will also be coordinating a research program that will keep her busy.

Life was supposed to be great for both of you with your big Academic achievements and for your dream to have a better life, but it has been the opposite. I can sense a bit of frustration with Ed. Ed wants the two of you to move to a place where you can find better opportunities. Ed, I can't blame you for feeling this way, but are you looking for positions for both of you or just for you? You seem to wonder why you have not gotten a full time position and your wife is making almost triple of your income. You cannot continue to wait for a better opportunity in the city you are in, whereas you have waited for four years for Ruby to finish. Even she did not apply for the job, it was offered to her. You, Ed, feel like "Mr. Idiot." You don't want to continue wasting your time. I know, Ed, life is like money, we are not supposed to waste it. Any time Ruby says something at home, you see her as a proud lady. To you, Ruby is not the lady you married. You see yourself as inferior to her.

I am wondering if you have been finding time to communicate. Perhaps you have been spending most of your time at home arguing, criticizing, blaming, and looking down on each other instead of talking to know the mind of each other. Even though, from Ruby's perspective, she is still the same Ruby to the best of her knowledge. She said she has been praying for you, Ed, for a better opportunity. She said she does appreciate your patience for her to finish her degree, and for being happy initially when she got her position at the university. She wants both of you to be working as a team; to be praying for a good opportunity for you and perhaps for both of you elsewhere. To her, she doesn't want to leave certainty for uncertainty. She'd rather go for a better position which will benefit both of you than a 50/50 percent opportunity.

I will like both of you to think beyond inferiority and superiority complexes. You need to see yourselves as one, as you have been before your big achievements. Academic degrees and big jobs or successes cannot replace joy or a happy marriage. Before your degrees, you were a happy couple, things were wonderful for you and people around you noticed these. Two years before Ed got his degree, both of you used to do things together, helping each other in all aspects of life.

Ruby loved her job, while Ed was looking forward to graduating and you were both happy when Ruby got admitted into her PhD program. What the devil is trying to use to separate you was supposed to unite you. The fact that at least one of you has a good job is good enough to make you thankful and be together looking for an opportunity for the second partner. You should try to come together as one and see each other's joy as both yours - and take the challenges of the second partner as both your challenges. Talk, pray and study the bible together and face the problem of inadequate job opportunities seriously. God wants you to have a happy relationship. God loves you and he cares for you as well.

Dear Ed & Ruby

Things seem to be getting worse for you. Ruby got a better and irresistible opportunity at a different university in another city. Ruby thinks she needs to accept the offer, while Ed is afraid of losing the little opportunity he has. The tension is so high in your home.

It is somehow difficult to know what to say. A good opportunity is not to be missed, but what about joy and harmony in your marriage? I am wondering how egocentrism will not take over your marriage. If care is not taken, your marriage will be controlled by an egotistic attitude. I will like both of you to see it as an opportunity cost. You have to forgo one thing for another. Although Ruby is of the opinion that her new income will be more than what both of you are currently making. It is a big job and a great opportunity for her as the chairperson of a research program in her new department. But what is that going to cost your marriage? If both of you are in agreement, it is a great opportunity. Otherwise, you have to pray about it and make sure that you are doing what God wants you to do. Ruby had already said yes to the offer. But can the university consider an opportunity for Ed in his field? Ruby, perhaps you can check with the university? Otherwise, Ed has to look into other universities in the city.

There should be more opportunities for him there than where you are now. A big city has a lot of opportunities and one of it is more universities – I believe there are four universities and two branches of two other universities. Prayerfully, Ed can get something for himself. But most importantly, you need to be one. God wants you to come to him as one body and one voice. With God all things are possible. Ed needs to forget about all the six years he has been looking for a better opportunity and believe that his time will soon come. Ed, your time is on the way. But before this prayer can be answered, you have to be in one spirit, one mind and one voice before God. Two cannot walk together unless they are in agreement (Amos 3:3). PhD degrees are supposed to brighten your relationship and not destroy it. There is great power in your agreements. Don't forget to make use of your God's lifetime warranty in your marriage, it will never expire.

You need to work on unconditional love and care. A Christian couple's love is supposed to be, "what is mine is yours, and what is yours is mine." But if egoism comes in, it is unlike Christ. God's unconditional nature of love is what is needed in your marital life. It may seem unrealistic for someone like Ed just to do whatever comes on the part of his wife or to go anywhere an opportunity takes his wife. Non-Christians believe something unusual may likely happen, when a wife has too much power or control. I don't think this is what supposed to be in your case. Whatever any child of God is or has is by the grace of God. None of you should allow egoism into your marital life. Make good use of the blessings of your Academic achievements to promote your marital love, and understanding. It's not about you, but about who gave you the opportunity to be what you are today.

If you decide to move let me know. I will be able to join you in prayer for a better position for Ed. God wants the best for your family and I do, too. Keep in touch, God bless you.

Dear Ruby & Ed

Greetings to you in the wonderful name of your greatest Counselor, Jesus Christ. I am happy that you were able to sell your house before you left and also able to buy a good house in your new city. Congratulations. Ruby likes her new job – it's challenging, but that's life. Ed, on the other hand, is just teaching one course, and stays home most of the time with your baby girl, who is ten months old. Being a stay at home dad is rewarding, even though it is not that easy. To you, Ed, life is stressful. You are thinking as if your life and Academic achievements are being wasted. Some of your mates are now full professors or in big positions at their workplaces. You seem to be angry.

As you have said Ed, you have gone to see all the Head of Departments in all the universities in the city and nothing is available for you. It seems as if you are regretting that you left your former university. A professor just left which would have been a good opportunity for you to replace him. You were actually thinking of applying for the position. But you are talking about four to five hour drive. Would you be going back and forth or coming home on weekends, or what? What about Rose, your daughter? Ruby is totally against your going back.

Financially speaking, it sounds great. But is it about the job and money or your home and marriage? One can have a good job and a bad home or marriage. As of now, the tension at home is higher than ever, all because of an inadequate job for Ed. Men always like to be the financial backbone in the homes, but anytime the situation is like that, what can one do? Is it possible for you to look for another part-time position in other universities? That is one of the opportunities of being in a bigger city with many universities. You can make good use of the opportunities. Perhaps you could also look for other opportunities with governments or agencies. I hope something good will come along your way.

Ed, you said that Ruby ignores you, most of the time, whenever she talks with her colleagues. She abandons you and talks with her 'people.' You said you always felt embarrassed and as if you are practically nothing. As such, you often don't feel like going to any party or functions with her, you're not even comfortable going to church because she speaks about her job with people or just talks with her colleagues at church – you always feel left out.

I am wondering what Ruby is thinking or what her defense is. God put us in the positions where we are to give glory to him. If what Ed has said is 100% true, I will like Ruby to be conscious of what Ed is angry about, even though Ruby is somewhat defensive. Don't allow jealousy to come between you and at the same time, the spirit of pride should not be tolerated. "Each of you should look not only to your own interest, but also the interests of others. Your attitudes should be the same as that of Christ Jesus who being in very nature of God did not consider equality with God...but made himself nothing, taking the very nature of a servant being made in human likeness...he humbled himself and he became obedient to death – even death on a cross! Therefore God exalted him to the highest place and gave him the name that is above every name, that at the name of Jesus every knee should bow in heaven and on earth and under the earth, and every tongue confess that Jesus Christ is Lord, to the glory of God the Father" (Phil. 2:4-11) (NIV). God wants both of you to be like Jesus. He doesn't want you to give any excuse for pride. God will help you. Keep in touch.

Dear Ruby & Ed

Thank you both for your telephone call. I am so concerned for your marriage and your well-being in general. This issue of no job for Ed has caused a lot of problems for your marriage. Many things seemed to be affected including your sexual life, communication, and your relationship has been really damaged. Ed has been sleeping in a different room and stopped going out with you, Ruby you also refuse to share news with him because you are afraid of being accused of pride and self-glorification.

If things continue like this, I wonder what the end of your marital life would likely be. If you stop sharing your bed or bedroom how can you have fun together in bed, including sexual intercourse. You are not sharing your bodies with each other. You are not sharing news – good or bad – with each other. Your communication seems nonexistent. You don't talk about your boy and girl. You hardly welcome each other home when one goes out. What kind of marital couple have you become? Love and care for each other are no longer there. You need to find a solution to these matters. They seem so serious. Your relationship is hurting. I am wondering if the children have been affected in one way or another.

Is there any possibility that other parties are involved in this case? Do you talk to friends a lot about the situations in your home? If yes, maybe you have to stop that. Perhaps your friends are counseling you wrongly. "I will never allow that to happen to me." "My wife/husband can never do or say that to me." "Don't be stupid, you are free to do or say whatever you want." "Education is a great liberator." "Don't let anyone or any situation enslave you." All these sayings and others are not more than what people can say to you. Do not be misled: "Bad Company corrupts good character" (1 Corinthians 15: 33) (NIV). Be careful of whom you seek opinion from or whom you share your stories with. Don't let unfaithful friends ruin your marriage.

I will like you to forget all the mess you are facing. Try to be one and find a job for Ed. The devil is happy for the offences between you and he is trying to accuse you before God whenever each one of you is praying. Resentment is there, bitterness is hidden somewhere. You should fight against division between you and pray for oneness. There is power in unity. United we stand, divided we fall. Try to have hope. You need to forget the past and dream together for the betterment of your family. As I said before, God's lifetime warranty in your marriage is still valid. It is time to use it. You have to go to the Lord on your knees together and ask for mercy. A united prayer will avail a lot. A prayer-less Christian is a power-less Christian. If you don't pray as one before God, you may not be able to achieve your goal. God wants to empower you. He wants you to be in unity so you will be able to defeat the devil. God is able to open a closed door for you. He knew that you would need a job, Ed, even before you received your PhD. Tell him to let you pass the obstacle before you. You need to get to the Promise Land. He parted the Red Sea for the Israelites, so he is able to open or clear the way for you to your destiny. Try to exercise faith in God and try to display faith because – "faith is being sure of what we hope for and certain of what we do not see" (Heb. 11:1) (NIV). Exercise faith diligently, God is able to surprise you. He is in control of every situation. He will answer those who diligently seek his face. Spend your weekend together in effectual prayers. God is willing to meet your needs. He is able. Amen.

Dear Ed & Rudy

I was thrilled to hear that Ed got a full-time position at a university very close to your house. That is Wonderful! The Psalm that came to mind when I got your note was Psalm 126. It says:

"When the LORD brought back the captive to Zion we were like man who dreamed. Our mouths were filled with laughter, our tongues with songs of joy. Then it was said among the nations, "The LORD has done great things for them." The LORD has done great things for us, we are filled with joy. Restore our fortunes, O LORD like streams in the Negev. Those who sow in tears will reap with songs of joy. He who goes out weeping, carrying seed to sow, will return with songs of joy, carrying sheaves with him" (NIV).

I am so happy for you, for all those years that you have been waiting. It is not easy to wait, but there is always a blessing afterward. As I'm rejoicing with you, I am also concerned for the damage that has been done during the time of waiting. There should be time for you to talk about those damages. You need to find time to talk about forgiveness on both sides. Let me know if you want me to write to you about what you need to do and the reasons why you need to forgive each other. I will certainly do so. As of now, I will like you to celebrate the blessing of a good job. The joy and happiness is not supposed to be just for Ed, but for the whole family. For now, try to forget about the past and rejoice together and let your children and friends know that you are happy. You should also try to improve your communication. I will not mind to write you about that, too.

Ed has a couple of weeks to go before he starts a different life. I believe he will not mind that. Although I am wondering how you are going to adjust to your schedule. Your little boy is under one year. You must have a good daycare around you. His sister is in school so that will be easier on you. You do not need to fold your hands with regards to talking to God. You should let him know that you really appreciate what he has done for you. You can demonstrate your appreciation to him in the way of worship or praise daily. I will encourage you not to be too busy to do your devotions – morning and evening – together. In fact, people, most of the time, move closer to God during trials and seem to give thanks or continue to talk to God whenever their requests are granted. The God of bad times is the God of good times. Praise him more at this time of joy. As you have been seriously talking to God for the past months, you should not forget that the devil is never on vacation. He is ready all the time to strike or fight back. You need to put on the full amour of God so that both of you will be able to take your stand against the devil's schemes (Eph. 6:11). I will encourage you to follow St. Paul's advice on how we can fight the devil in the rest of the chapter. Please find time not only to read but also to meditate and put into practice Paul's revelation in (Eph.6:10-20).

I will be waiting to hear from you to know if you want me to write to you about forgiveness and communication. If you have any other topic in mind, let me know. I wish you all the best, and I hope you will accept my congratulatory message. Keep in touch. God bless you richly.

Dear Ruby & ED

You are both busy in a good way. I am happy for you. Your children must have also realized the difference in you. It was also nice to hear that Ed had a good start and the students seem to like him. You wanted me to talk about forgiveness, even though I've made reference to it a few times, in my letters to you and during our telephone conversations.

It was God himself who initiated forgiveness. And he wanted us to pass it on to each other or one another. In your own case, it is supposed to be simple. The bone of contention is over. But the damages may want to hang around for a while, if care is not taken. To begin with, both of you need to humble yourselves before God. You should not feel too big to apologize to each other and when apology takes place, the other party needs to let go and let God. When offences are not pardoned, peace, joy etc. would be missing, bitterness may likely kick in and anger and frustration will find their rooms in the particular person. When all these are present, the possibility of hatred will be there and that would lead to fighting and lack of trust would ensue. But if we can let go of our angers toward the offender, we are not only doing him/her a favor, we do ourselves a big favor, too.

Joseph in the Old Testament had a big reason not to forgive his brothers, after all the hatred they had shown to him. They sold him into slavery – even though God turned their evil into positive outcome for Joseph – he ended up in prison. I would imagine that he was not bitter toward them at that time. Perhaps God quickly honored Joseph in line with what Joseph had seen about his destiny. He became second in command in the Egyptian government. His brothers went to him to buy food. He later on declared his identity to them. The brothers were thinking that he would take revenge on them, but Joseph, as a man of God, forgave his brothers (Gen. 45).

My suggestion to you, Ruby, is to learn from Joseph and try to forgive Ed. Try to celebrate the good news or the blessing of a new job. Ed should not feel too big – proud – to apologize. Many people always like to hear 'I am sorry' from the one who offended them. Ed, 'I am sorry' is a very simple sentence, but it is not always easy to utter for many people. Tell Ruby that you are sorry; you don't need to defend yourself but ask for forgiveness. Promise her, if you think it fit, that you will no longer be abusive to her. You are happy now. Thank God that during the issues you were able to pray together. God honored himself. He answered your prayers. You have to say thank you to him by forgiving each other. Ruby, you, too, need to apologize to Ed and both of you have to live out the words of the Lord's prayer, "... and forgive us our sins as we have forgiven those who sin against us." (Matt. 6:12) (NLT).

Both Jesus and Stephen prayed to God to forgive their enemies (Luke 23:34; Acts. 7:60). I will invite both of you to join Jesus and Stephen to pray to God to help you forgive each other and to let go of the past. There is nothing you can do about it, you cannot take the past back, but you should learn from it. Let me know what you think about forgiveness. God bless you.

Dear Ed & Ruby,

Greetings to you and your children. Yes, you are right to say that your test produced a testimony. You have been telling your friends and your colleagues how you prayed through Ed's unemployment. You have been telling them the importance of prayer and that they should not make prayer their last resort in times of need and that it should be their first priority. You are doing well. Trials are supposed to improve us not to dispose us. It is opposite for the devil. He brings trials to Christians to make us bitter and angry toward God.

Well, this is part of what I wanted to talk about. Communication! When we pray, we communicate with God, while he does the same with us when we read his words – the bible. We need both. Even though your communication has been improving in recent months, for the past years, it has been bad. You need to find time out of no time to have effective communication with each other. You should share your joys and difficulties together. You have a lot to talk about; your children's successes and failures, your parents on both sides, how your workplace or colleagues are treating you etc. You should communicate in plain language. No Winner or loser in a good marital communication, talk with each other with clarity, don't talk for or think for each other. That is to say, there should be no assumptions that she/he knows or should know. Many wives or husbands believe wrongly that since they know the subject or what they are talking about, their spouses are supposed to know it as well.

Both verbal and nonverbal communications are very important in any successful marriage. You ought to find time to have fun together and to celebrate one of God's most powerful gifts to marriage. God wants all marital couples to improve their relationship, to love each other, to verbalize their love for each other and also to communicate their love for each other romantically. Sexual intercourse should not be underrated in your marital life. As you have admitted, you have not been doing very well sexually in the past years. It is time for you to redeem the past. Verbal and nonverbal communications need to be increased in your marriage. Don't be too busy to talk and to appreciate each other. Do things together and include your children sometimes. You ought to dream together and work out how to accomplish your dreams. There is always a bigger power in working together than in division.

The two of you will most likely be busier than before, don't forget, you asked for it. Whenever you complain that you don't have time to communicate with God or for him to communicate with you, or you don't have time to communicate with each other – both verbal and nonverbal – you are trying to blame God for giving Ed a full time position. Before God gave Ed a job, he trusted you that you can handle and balance both your jobs and communications. The devil always tries to deceive Christians that they don't have enough time to pray, to read God's words or to have quality time with their marital partner. Don't let him deceive you as he has been doing with many children of God. He is a liar and a manipulator, and he's still using the same old tactics he used with Adam and Eve (Gen.3). There are many battles to be won through communication. I believe God will give you all you need to be a great couple and great professors. Talk to him about everything including your jobs. God bless you.

Dear Ruby & Ed,

Thank you for sharing all the good news with me. It has been a while, since I wrote last. I am happy that things are well with you. You have purchased a new house and you have paid 50% of the cost. Ed has been given an acting chair of research position in his department and Ruby is now a full professor. Your children are excelling in school and in their sports activities. You have so many things to celebrate. I believe that you have been praising God for his kindness to you. His praise should come naturally whenever you count your blessings. Do not stop praising and worshiping him. He is so good to you. I am also happy that the past is behind you now. You had a long weekend to talk about your past and apologize to each other. You took a step further and engaged in prayers of forgiveness and reconciliation for each other. You have been having good and effective communication including nonverbal communication, that is, your sexual exercise has increased dramatically. It is good to know!

I am wondering if you know any couples among your friends or colleagues who are having similar problems you had. God saves us to serve others and to be a blessing to others. There are opportunities for you to reach out to people who are in the situation you have experienced. The time you spent to pray together and talk with good friends for encouragement and prayers were not in vain. I hope you will not be saying: "We are lucky," and stop there. I know you are blessed, but God blessed you so that you will be able to bless others. I mean to say that you need to allow God to bless others through you. It can happen. Let people thank God for helping them to overcome their rough time caused by lack of good jobs. God is able to use anyone, I hope you will say: "Here we are, use us Lord."

The devil wanted to ruin your marriage. God was so good to rescue you from marriage failure. But guess what? The devil is a stubborn foe, he doesn't get defeated easily. But the good news is the same God who had enabled you to defeat him, is still in the business of overcoming the devil over and over again. Do not rest; try to be offensive and not defensive. I mean, don't wait for a trial before you attack him every-day through powerful prayers and deepening yourselves in the words of God. There are so many life storms, but we Christians are not alone. Christ is fighting for us all the time. The battle is not ours, it is the Lord's. Continue to be prayerful and dedicated in your faith. The devil was defeated 2000 plus years ago, so victory is yours. But you don't need to fold your hands, do what is in your power and let God do his part. Victory is ours all the time.

It has been a good experience to be working with you for the past years. I learnt a lot from you. I know how any incident can change things around for better or for worse. *I am also reminded* from your story that we don't need to be discouraged, when there is hope there is life not just the usual saying; when there is life there is hope. Try to be strong in the Lord, continue to be one. Unity is your strength. Don't let the enemy – the devil – come in-between you. Above all, let your request be made known to God. May the Lord of peace grant you peace, joy, and love for each other. Thank you for your openness. God bless you all the time.

Chapter 10
Sola and Emily – Intermarriage (Culture Clash)

Dear Sola & Emily,

It was nice to hear from you and that you got my phone number from a doctor's office. I hope you are doing well. Let me recap what you said about your marital challenges. Sola, when you were dating Emily, your parents were not too keen about it. They were wondering how cultural difference would not be a problem in your relationship. However, to you and Emily, love is greater than culture. You loved each other and you got married.

Your problem started before your wedding, Sola's parents expected Emily to address them as Mr. & Mrs., while Emily's parents wanted to be called by their first names. You waited for two years before you started raising children; Sola's parents called so many times to ask when you were going to start your family. When you had your first baby, Emily's mom just stayed for one week and her dad came for two days, while Sola's dad stayed for two weeks and his mom wanted to stay for months until you told her to go after two months. She was upset and started to wonder how her daughter-in-law could have driven her away from her son's house.

Sola's parents desire a monthly allowance and also want Emily to greet them with respect by curtsying/kneeling for them like they do in the Yoruba culture. Sola's brothers and sisters love to come and spend their vacations with you, sometimes without any approval from you. Whenever any of Sola's people – family – come to visit, they always want to eat their native dish and want it on time.

I am wondering how all these issues are making you feel? What is going on in your mind? I am not sure, if you've had the time to share you cultures, especially Sola. How much of your culture did you share with Emily? In your culture, Sola, your wife is not just your wife, she is a wife to many people. I believe you know what I am talking about. The only control a couple in your culture has is no one can share a bed with the wife. The wife is supposed to serve her husband's family with good food and care for them, perhaps more than her husband. The parents of the groom always expect complete respect from their daughter-in-law. And when you are not ready for a baby, you should not be ready for a wedding. No child in the first year of marriage means something is wrong with the couple. Some parents of the groom would like their son to be given them monthly allowance or gifts. The house of the groom, to his parents and siblings is "our" house and the parents of the groom believe they have the right to stay with their grandchildren until they feel like leaving. Anything contrary to that is a problem, even though educated parents would understand better than the unlettered parents.

So Emily and Sola, the problems you are having are not so bad, perhaps it is a culture shock! What can you do about the conflicts? I will suggest to Emily to familiarize herself with the Yoruba culture. If possible, you can find books on Yoruba culture to read. First of all, your dating was too short. Six months courtship was not long enough for Emily to visit Yoruba families in your cities, and perhaps to visit Sola's parents many times. When you were dating, love was blind. You did not ask or talk about what your families would expect from you, and what your experiences with both families may be like. Sola, try to explain your culture to Emily. If you cannot find books on Yoruba culture let me know. God bless you.

Dear Sola and Emily,

I am happy to hear that you have been talking about the differences between the Yoruba – African - and western culture. Sola also found it odd to call his parents-in-law by their first names as well as Emily's Aunts and Uncles. This is un-Yoruba. But you said you are getting used to it. It is easier for you, Sola, to get used to it because you see it every day. When you were in the university, many of your professors preferred to be called by their first names, also some of your bosses at work wanted you to call them by their first names. Emily doesn't see that very often, that is, calling almost everybody Mr. or Mrs. or by their other titles.

Sola ordered a book for you from his homeland. That's great! How are you enjoying it? Both of you described your last three years of marriage as almost "hell". Don't worry, things will be alright and perhaps you will be able to use more positive words, like heavenly, to describe your marriage soon, once you find your way around Sola's culture.

If there are Yoruba clubs in your city, I will suggest that you try to attend their meetings or functions, so that you can quickly familiarize yourself with Sola's culture. You can also be visiting Yoruba couples and families. You can also try to forget all that Sola's parents have done to you and try to have a visit with them during your vacation. Spend at least two weeks with them, humble yourself as you relate to his mom. Tell her to explain some of the things that are odd to you. Ask her how she feels about having a white daughter-in-law. This is not about racism, but about cultural differences. She also has been in the western world for about six years now. Maybe she, too, is trying to identify with your culture. Don't feel shy to talk with her. Let her know that you are not a proud person, but not familiar with her cultural practices. Apologize to her and to Sola's dad, too, if need be. Perhaps they, too, will be able to ask for forgiveness on your own part. As children of God, all of you are supposed to remember that we all share one culture, that is, a heavenly culture. The Apostle Paul reminds us: "You are all sons of God through faith in Christ Jesus, for all of you who were baptized into Christ have clothed yourselves with Christ. There is neither Jew nor Greek, Slave nor free, male nor female, for you are all one in Christ Jesus. If you belong to Christ, then you are Abraham's seed, and heirs according to the promise" (Gal 3:26-29) (NIV).

Cultural differences should not be a big deal for all of you since you are Christians. You are of one family – Abraham's family and God's culture. Sola, you have to be careful not to judge your parents or accuse them of causing problems in your marriage. I believe they love you and they want to love your wife at the same time. Encourage them to talk with both of you about Yoruba culture, when they are directly teaching Emily, perhaps you, too, can pick up some new teachings, or you can refresh your memories about some forgotten norms. If need be, you can talk to Emily's parents about what you consider to be challenges in their culture. You have a long way to go – your children are getting older; how are you going to bring them up? I will address this with you as time goes by. Let's see how you will make out with regards to talking to your parents on both sides. Let me about the outcome.

Dear Emily & Sola,

Wow, you spent two weeks and three days with Sola's parents. Emily, you said it was like being in school. You learnt a lot and now understand where your in-laws were coming from. They wanted their grandchildren to share some Yoruba values with regards to culture. They were afraid that you may not likely let that happen. They verbalized it to you for the first time in the past five years. But it was really good to know that Sola's mom called you "iyawo mi" (my wife). And on your own side, you were able to say some words in Sola's language for the first time, words like: *e pele o* (hello); *e kabo* (welcome); *o dabo* (goodbye); *o daro* (good night); *e se o* (thank you).

I am very impressed with you, Emily. Your in-laws were very happy with you and they laughed a lot with you. The barrier between you and them has been broken. I hope each time they call or you call them, you will be able to say *e pele o* (hello) and after your conversation you will say *o daro o* (good night) or *o dabo o* (good bye). Do whatever you can to make your new relationship go smoothly. They seem to be nice in-laws to be with. Sola didn't have much to learn as far as language is concerned, he had been learning for the past twenty-five years. But if there are some western cultures you are not familiar with, you should talk to your in-laws. If both of you really want to enjoy your marital life, you have to be friendly with your in-laws. Emily, as I mentioned earlier, you are blessed to have in-laws who can speak the English language. The situation could have been worse. Do not hesitate to ask any questions from your in-laws. And any time they come to visit, give them the chance to tell you when they want to leave. If it is you that invites them for a visit, tell them how long you are inviting them for. For instance, one of you can call and tell them you would like them to come and visit for a week or that you would like them to come and visit or play with their grandchildren for one or two weeks. If they come and want to stay longer than you had proposed to them, then you have the right to say no with genuine reasons.

Since the bone of contention is mended, you have to make sure that you build upon the good foundation you have laid. You have to let go of the past. I will be talking about this later. Try to refresh your memories on what tried to break your marital relationship apart. The Yoruba words that Emily has acquired should not just die. Sola, you should let Emily say them occasionally. Whenever unity stands, division must fall.

Try to make yourselves one. Cultures should not separate you. Whatever God has joined together, cultures should not put asunder. You loved each other and that was the reason you got married, let your reason or reasons for marrying each other stand. God loves you and that stands forever. May he continue to bless your marriage. Keep in touch.

Dear Sola & Emily,

Greetings. I understood that Emily's parents were wondering why both of you are spending more time with Sola's parents than with them. They complained that you spent 17 days with Sola's parents while you only spent a couple of days with them. They believe that "all animals are equal." And felt that Sola's parents compelled Emily to learn and speak Yoruba. The tension between you started all over again. Each one of you is wondering why you entered into this kind of mess – that you got married to a person of a different culture and language.

I can sense your frustration. How are you trying to solve the problems? Emily, did you explain to your parents that you learned Sola's language out of your willingness and not compulsion? If you have not explained the situation to them, it will be better that you do. Sola cannot do it for you, it would look like he is trying to defend his parents. Try to let them know that you love your husband and that was the reason you married him and you don't want anything – big or small – to ruin your relationship. You want to do whatever is in your power to save you marriage. You learnt Yoruba language for better communication between you and your Parents in-law. Let them also know that you speak the language with any Yoruba person you see around – you enjoy saying the words like e pele o (hello); o dabo o (good bye) and so on...

At the same time, Emily's parents are right. Since you stayed so long with Sola's parents, you should have let them know why you went and that you will stay with them for a long period of time on your vacation next year. They also deserve to see their grandchildren for more than a couple of days on each visit. Perhaps you need to start to rotate your vacations or holidays like Easter, Thanksgiving and Christmas. The parents on both sides would be happy to see that you are not one sided. Equal treatments are good for both of them. The two of you and the children should plan to spend a long weekend with your parents, Emily. Don't wait till the problem escalates before you do something about it. I know, it has become an issue between you, but don't let it become bigger than it is.

I believe that there are no traces of racism in the matter on both sides. I asked you before, but you said no. If no is still the answer to the question, what I will suggest to you is to invite both of them for a big holiday – Easter, Thanksgiving or Christmas. They need to know one another better. I don't think they know one another well. Be smart. Make them friends. If they like one another, your family will benefit from it a lot. To come for a holiday is not just for a day trip. I mean, they should stay for at least three or four days with you. If you agree, try it and see how it will work out.

I can only imagine what is going on in your minds before you start to wonder why you got married to each other. I believe you told me before that you were convinced that God's hands were in your marriage. You both prayed for months before you said yes to each other. If your marriage is from God, his helping hands are there to help you. The tension will soon be over. It is one of the marital trials that many marital couples face. Take it easy. Slowly, but surely, the problems will be over. Take it to God, since he knew your different cultures before he allowed you to get married. He must have a way out for you. Don't be frustrated, because that will make the devil happy. Thank God for your marriage and commit it into his everlasting hands. He is always there to help. Keep in touch. God bless you.

Dear Emily & Sola,

That must have been a wonderful Thanksgiving. Your parents from both sides came and spent 5 days with you. They all enjoyed themselves. Both moms helped in the kitchen with the preparations of Thanksgiving dinner. Wonderful! The four of them laughed a lot. They talked for hours each day. You heard Emily's mom say: "E se o" (thank you) and "o dabo" (good bye). They even planned to exchange visits in the future. Good. In the process of talking, they realized that they knew some of the same people. They asked you to do it again. Your children loved to have all their four grandparents together. They had fun with all of them.

I want to check from you if you are trying to speak some Yoruba language with your children. It will also be beneficial for both your children and Sola's parents, if the children can be exposed to both languages and cultures. I know they may not be able to speak Yoruba language fluently, but it will be good for them, if they can understand basic and even say some words. Try to teach them not to be ashamed of Yoruba (African) culture, even though it may not be easy for them to embrace it. For example, I believe their paternal grandparents will be happy, if their grandchildren can greet them with some respect, not to try to shake hand with them, but to prostrate and kneel down - boy and girl, respectively. You don't need to make it compulsory but try to explain to them why they need to be familiar with both cultures.

When Jesus was young, he was exposed to the Jewish culture. He participated in all cultural festivals and followed his parents – even though Joseph was not his biological father. He used to eat any food available at home or culturally served. It will be great, if your children can have interest in some Yoruba – Nigerian –cuisine. Although I do not know, if Sola's parents eat Nigerian or African foodstuff – like iyan, eba, black eye beans etc–if they do, they will appreciate it, if their grandchildren can have a taste of their grandma's dishes. Do not be offended, if the children refuse to eat or do not eat it well.

You asked of my thoughts with regards to church attendance. It seems that Sola likes an African church where the children will be able to associate with other black children. I will like to suggest that you discuss that among yourselves and decide what you should do. God is the same in black or white churches. A good church where the gospel is preached is the most important. Make sure you find a good church with sound doctrine. Many churches today are neglecting the true doctrine centered on Jesus Christ's virgin birth, the death and resurrection of Jesus Christ. As long as the church you attend is a bible-based church, it is okay. For the point of the children to be exposed to many black children, it may be okay to visit a black church once in a while. I will leave the final decision with you.

Above all, I will like to advise you to train your children in a godly way, the book of proverbs says: "Train a child in the way he should go, and when he is old he will not depart from it" (Prov.22:6) (NIV). This is not because they are black or 50/50, but it is ideal to do so for all children. Train them to pray, to love reading the Scripture and to like going to church. Both of you ought to lead by example. Continue to be godly parents. Whatever they learn from you will remain with them forever. God bless you.

Dear Emily & Sola,

Compliment of the season. It is nice to know that you and the children are doing fine. The children are picking some words in Yoruba language and are trying hard to eat some Nigerian food. I hope you will continue the good job with the children.

Another challenge, the children have been facing are issues of discrimination at school. The black students do not really associate themselves with your children, because they are not as black as them. The white students are saying something similar to that. So your children are not having many students to play with. Thank God that they have a couple of friends who do not care about color. I am wondering how the children are feeling about that. What have you done so far about it? You see, children are very honest; sometimes they just say something as it occurs to them. They don't have the opportunity to ponder on what they want to say before they say it.

I suggest that you talk to your children and tell them not to be offended about that, and also not to be fed up or hate school because of the situation. Let them be advised that they are as equal as any "real black" or "real white" student in the school, also God sees your children as important to him like anyone else. Let them know that they are very unique like all children. They should not look down on themselves, but to work well in order to impress their teachers. Have you talked to their teachers as well as the principal or administration about the issue? If not, why not? The children go to a public school and the school is supposed to be for everyone. I do understand that we cannot impose friendship on anyone conversely it will be unjust for young children like yours to be exposed to discrimination. You have to work hard to see that it will not continue for long.

At the same time, I will discourage you from using sensitive words like racism, injustice, even discrimination. I hope the school is not using those words for the children. However, if there is any trace of racism, you should try to quickly do something about it. It should not go so far. I doubt it, when you were dating, if you ever thought that you would be facing all these kinds of nasty issues. I am not sure, if you have also been facing any similar issues like that when people see you together as a married couple. Well, it is too late. You are there already. You can't get out of your marriage because of minor problems you have been facing.

Let the problems you have been facing bring you close and closer. The good news is; there is no white, black, red or otherwise in heaven. There is no partiality with God. He does not prefer any color. Be there for your children, they should not run away from school. I hope as time goes on, they will be able to have many friends and continue to love school. By the way, do they like their teachers? God bless you all. Tell the children that God loves them.

Dear Sola & Emily,

Thank you for your telephone calls. I am glad to know that things are getting better for your children. You went to the school to talk with their teachers and the principal. You have done a great job. I hope life will be getting better and better. I wish them all the best and trust that they will be having more and more friends.

Sola, Emily complained that you always have fun talking in Yoruba anytime your parents visit or both of you go to them. She also said that you do the same thing, in her presence, whenever you see any Yoruba person or when you're in the midst of Yoruba people. Whenever you and other Yorubas are talking, you laugh aloud most of the time. Sola, if you were Emily, how would you feel? You need to do to others as you would have them do to you (Luke 6: 31). She does not understand what you and others – including your parents –are saying in your language, so how can she be sure that you were not talking about her, since she was not included in your discussion? I am sure that if you had taken time to explain to her what you were talking about when alone, she wouldn't have been so offended.

I will like to advise that each time you are talking with any Yoruba person who understands or speaks English, try to speak the language Emily would be able to follow and if she wishes, she can also contribute to your conversations. You should not give the devil any chances. You don't have to tell people who are speaking to you in Yoruba to speak English, you can easily respond to them in English. After you do that in a few sentences, others may likely change to English. You can tell your parents, brothers and sisters to speak to you in English whenever Emily is around for the sake of peace between you and your wife.

Both of you have to establish trust in each other. If you trust each other, there would be no misunderstanding or suspicion. Emily, you need to believe that your husband would not say anything bad about you. If love is there between you, things are supposed to be fine. Listen to what love is: "Love is patient, love is kind. It does not envy, it does not boast, it is not proud. It is not rude, it is not self-seeking, it is not easily angered; it keeps no record of wrongs. Love does not delight in evil but rejoices with the truth. It always protects, always trusts, always hopes, always perseveres" (I Cor. 13:4-7) (NIV).

Let your love for each other enable you to trust and protect each other. God has you on his agenda. He always carries you along with himself. Try to be like him, carry each other along with yourself. Above all, let your marriage commitment and love supersede other small issues that the devil can use as tools to dissolve your marital relationship. Your marriage is greater than your culture or languages. Pray for each other and pray together, study the word of God together and allow it to guide you and to be your focus in your marital life. God loves you and so do I. Keep in touch. God bless you.

Dear Emily & Sola,

You are a nice couple to work with. You always follow my advice. Sola has improved himself by speaking in English while talking to his parents or other Yorubas whenever you are there, Emily. That was a good sense of compassionate love. However, you still need to keep working on what you have been doing well.

If you can remember, I tried to write you about the importance of forgiveness, effective communication, commitment and love. I also told you that God's purpose for your marriage should be greater than the differences of your cultures and languages. When you were dating each other, you had love for yourselves, greater than the differences between you. In fact, all you need to do is spend your energy on what brought you together. I will believe the will of God or his divine purpose joined you together. Don't waste your time on what can divide you, but on what can make your marital stability stronger. You need to replenish your agape love – real love, unconditional love. If the agape love is the center of your marriage, the rest is a piece of cake.

As God had forgiven each one of you – while we were yet sinners Christ died for us (Rom. 5:8; I Pet. 4:10) – you need to extend grace to each other. If your grace – unmerited gift – for each other increases, your accusations will decrease. The apostle Paul urges: "The law was added so that the trespass might increase. But where sin increased, grace increased all the more, so that, just as sin reigned in death, so also grace might reign through righteousness to bring eternal life through Jesus Christ our Lord" (Rom 5:20-21) (NIV). Paul was correct.

You need also to continue practicing effective communication. Talk loud and clear with each other. Don't leave a stone untouched- don't think anything is unimportant to talk about. Nothing is too big or too small for a marital couple to talk about. If anything bothers you, talk about it. Bear each other's burden. That is what marriage is all about. God said many years ago in the first story of marital life, "it is not good for a man to be alone." He did not stop there, he further said, "I will make him a helper, a suitable mate for him" (Gen. 2:18) (NIV). God said the same thing to you, Sola. He made Emily for you as your helper and suitable mate for you. When you love each other daily, you are trying to demonstrate your appreciation to God. Thank him every second by loving and caring for each other.

It is a very great opportunity to know you. You are a great couple. God loves you. He will not leave you alone. He will help you work together as a team. Only the black keys of a piano cannot work by themselves without white keys. When both black and white keys are played together, it always result in good music. The same will happen to you, if you co-operate. Be blessed in the Lord.

Chapter 11
Bev and Les – Unequal Yoke
(How to Handle Religious Issues)

Dear Bev

I greet you in the name of Jesus, the King of kings and Lord of lords. I am glad to hear that one of your friends referred you to me. It was nice to talk to you on the phone the other day. This letter is to fulfill my promise. Let me recap what you said on the phone. Les, your husband, has no religion. He doesn't go to church with you, and he doesn't like to see you reading the bible, you are not allowed to pray aloud in the house, especially praying in Jesus' name. Nobody from church is allowed to visit you and also it has been a big fight for you to visit your Christian friends. Whenever you go to church, you have to rush home because Les always gets frustrated when you are out for more than two hours on Sundays. There's no opportunity for you to attend mid-week programs at church. Your involvement in church is limited to Sunday services.

You wanted to join the choir or prayer team, but Les said no. He allowed your two kids to go to Sunday school before, but he stopped them a couple of months ago. The kids were crying and they cry every Sunday morning, but Les prefers to take them to the park or to a movie, and that was what he has been doing with the children. The situation is moving from bad to worse. You have been pushed to the wall. You still love him; you believe he is a good provider and a good father to your children. But he has more or less imprisoned you as far as Christianity is concerned.

You said you were raised in a Christian home and you met the Lord in a deeper way when you were in university. I am wondering how much you knew about Les when you met him or while you were dating. I think you must have been familiar with what the apostle Paul said about what is happening to you now. He urged: "Do not be yoked with unbelievers. For what do righteousness and wickedness have in common? Or what fellowship can light have with darkness? What harmony is there between Christ and Belial? What does a believer have in common with unbeliever? What agreement is there between the temple of God and idols? For we are the temple of the living God" (2 Cor.6:14-16) (NIV). Certainly, Paul's admonition must make more sense to you now.

I am wondering how much your parents, your Christian friends or your pastor know about the situation in your home. As you have said, you love Les, and that he is a good provider for you and the children. I will urge you to increase your time of prayer for him. Tell mom and dad to join you in praying for him. Your pastor should know and start to intercede for God's breakthrough for Les to give you freedom to worship or he himself to come to Christ. Les can stop you from praying aloud, but he cannot stop you from praying silently for him. God hears audible prayers as well as silent prayers. Paul the apostle addressed your circumstances many years ago. He advises: "And if a woman has a husband who is not a believer and he is willing to live with her, she must not divorce him. For the unbelieving husband has been sanctified through his believing wife. Otherwise, your children would be unclean, but as it is, they are holy. But if the unbeliever leaves, let him do so. A believing man or woman is not bound in such circumstances; God has called us to live in peace" (I Cor. 7:13-15) (NIV). It happened to early Christians, you're not alone. God will see you through.

You and Les have been living together for the past 7 years. The only complaint you have against him is your lack of freedom to worship. That is a big issue, but it's not bigger than what Jesus can handle. You can discipline yourself by praying and fasting. For sure, God will intervene. I will join you in prayers, too. Let him see Christ in you more than before. God bless you.

Dear Bev,

Thank you for your comments over the phone. I am delighted that you have been praying for him. You have been fasting three days a week, but Les does not know. When you both arrive home from work you always have supper with the family. Your parents were a bit upset with you that you have been suffering in silence. But they are praying with you, believing that God will do something about it. Your parents and Christian friends have been praying for your religious freedom and for God to speak to Les. It is good to know all of these.

Have you ever considered talking to Les' parents and his siblings about your situation? Les' mom is a churchgoer. His dad goes occasionally, but he has no problem with Les' mom going to church. All of Les' three brothers and sister attend church. His mom may likely understand your position. You don't need to tell them or her as if you are reporting their brother/son, but to tell them so that they can join you in prayer. You can lay more emphasis on Les' refusal to let the children attend Sunday school. His dad never restricted his children from going to Sunday school or to church with their mom. Let us wait and see what his siblings and parents, especially his mom, will do or say to him.

Another step you can prayerfully consider is to talk with him about how you are feeling regarding his refusal to let the children go to Sunday school. If you agree to talk with him, I will suggest that you do it in a romantic way. If you are financially capable, you can go away for a weekend. You may invite his mom to babysit for you. Get away and try to be good to him. Plan to have fun in a romantic way. Sometimes on Saturday, you can tell him in a very polite way, not in a judgmental way. Do not accuse him or make him feel guilty for not being too open with your religious freedom, especially for the children. Humbly beg him to let you be more involved in church and for the children to attend church with you. If you say yes to this idea, you have to pray hard about it and tell all your prayer partners to join you in prayers. Tell them what your plans are.

I will like you to remember that with God all things are possible (Luk.1:37). God wants us to make our request known to him. The apostles might have prayed a lot for people like Saul who later on became Paul. Paul was one of the biggest enemies of the cross. But when God arrested him, God did not only change Paul, but he equipped him for the work of God's kingdom. When Stephen was about to be stoned to death, Saul was there (Acts 7:58). Saul gave the approval for Stephen's death and he began to destroy the Church of Christ. He started to go from house to house. He put many of Christ's followers in the prison (Acts 8:1-3). What changed Saul were the effective prayers of the believers and the loving attitude toward him and others. Stephen even prayed "...Lord, do not hold this sin against them" (Acts 7:60) (NIV). God in his mightiness arrested Saul and converted him and he became an indispensable witness for Christ in the New Testament.

Let that attitude of the apostles be also in you. And if God can change the enemy of the Cross to a powerful friend and defender of the Cross, he is able to do so in the life of Les. God is the same yesterday, today and forever (Heb.13:8). Jesus loves you. He knows what you are going through. He has a way out for you. Don't be discouraged. God will make you laugh over the situation. By the way, is Les aware that you have been talking with me? God bless you.

Dear Bev,

It was great to know that you went on a date with Les a couple of weekends ago. The hotel was along the beach. You took a long walk on the beach and had fun on the white sand. You had long discussions on the religion issue. His mom asked the children in their dad's presence how they were making out in Sunday school and the children replied that they had not been going. His mom pretended as if she did not know anything, and she asked you why the children have not been attending Sunday school. But you did not say much. That was a smart idea. Before you went away for the weekend, Les told you of his interest in a particular religion. Some of his coworkers have been trying to witness to him at work.

Les told you why he did not have interest in religion or lost his taste for it. He used to go to Sunday school with his mom, but when he got to university and saw that many of his friends were not interested in church and that some professors were anti-religion, he felt inadequate to tell his friends that he was interested in religion so he got lost in the crowd. Since then, Les has not attended church. And most of the time, he holds the opinion that God does not exist. You had a deep discussion about God's existence and his power to do all things. You also spoke about the importance of prayer and God's ability to answer prayer. You told him how many times you prayed and God answered. You ended up praying together. You were surprised to hear him say amen, at the conclusion of your prayer.

It was good the way you handled your weekend. Les agreed that you should resume taking the kids to Sunday school. But he did not agree that you can go to church during the week or join the choir. I hope you will not worry yourself too much about that. You had a good weekend and God was on your side. Do not be discouraged, you have covered a lot of ground. Don't fold your arms or be disappointed that you did not get everything. Remember, Rome was not built in a day. You are far better where you are now than before your weekend getaway.

Perhaps if there are any good programs or activities pertaining to Christianity in the city, you can ask him, if he would like to go with you. Also, if you can pick up good books about faith in Jesus, you can discuss interesting aspects of the book(s) with him. Slowly, but surely, you will get to where you are going. But if you are in a hurry, it may lead you back to square one. By God's grace, you will get to where you want to be. Take it easy, God knows what you are going through. And he has a way out. As I've said before, you need to be as patient as possible. You have a double role to play in Les' life. You are his wife and a missionary to him. You have to understand where he is coming from. He has been influenced by a wrong crowd. If a group of people can change his mind as far as Christianity is concerned, you, too, can do the same. You can get him back from their hands and lead him back to the Cross. With God on your side, all things are possible.

You said you told Les about me. How do you think he will feel if I write both of you together or to him separately? Before I do that, we have to increase our prayers for him. As soon as he knows that I am a Christian counselor, he may not feel comfortable, but if we can make our requests known to God, he knows what to do. Just continue to represent Jesus Christ well in his life. Let the beauty of Christ be seen in you and ask Jesus whatever you want God to do in his life. Jesus said that whatever we ask in his name from his Father would be granted unto us (John 14:13-14). Do so and get the answer. Keep in touch. God bless you.

Dear Bev,

I am positive that God is on your side. The children have been attending Sunday school and Les has been more open to religious conversations. You mentioned that some guys came to your home and talked with Les about their religion and they conducted some kind of ritual with Les. He doesn't know how to say no to these guys because one of them is Les' boss. Les seems to be confused about religion. He is a man of two islands.

You have two battles facing you. The good news is that the battles are not yours. Christ fought and won the battles for you more than two thousand years ago. While on the cross, He said: "It is finished" (John 19:30) (NIV). You need to allow Jesus to help you out. Try not to fight Les. In fact, you did a good job by entertaining his friends after their ceremony. You have to continuously pray against division between you and Les. Those guys and religion have no right to separate what God himself has joined together. God, the author and finisher of your faith and your marriage agreed that the two of you are one since both of you said "I do." God is still saying today with regard to your marriage that what He has joined together, let no man or men, religion or whatsoever separate (Mk 10:9). The soul of anyone or everybody is in the hands of our Lord Jesus Christ. God knows how to touch Les and witness to or convict him. He is not too far away from God's reach, and he also knows how to stop anyone or any situation that may ruin your marriage. I believe God knew that a time like this was coming. Life may seem unfair, but God is fair. He is also good. What you see as impossible is possible for God, with him, anything is possible. Christian faith teaches unconditional love. There's nothing greater you can do for Les than to demonstrate your love to him. God is love that is his attribute. God loves you. I believe you love him, too. Let God know that you love Les through the agape-unconditional- love you show to him, and also to those who want to separate you and Les through their religion. However, don't let their religion ruin your marriage. I know they seem to be powerful and wealthy, but your Jesus is the most powerful and wealthiest you can ever imagine. Don't let your heart be troubled (John 14:1). Cast all your anxiety upon Christ, he cares for you (I Pet. 5:7).

I strongly believe that your husband is not totally against Christianity or God, since he allowed your kids to return to Sunday school. He occasionally joins you in prayers, and you said that he went to church with you on Easter Sunday, and he also went to the last Christmas Eve service with you. He is not too far away from salvation. Don't give in and don't give up as well. You said his dad and mom sent him a copy of a study guide bible. You've seen him reading it sometimes. Don't pressurize him to read it, but at the same time, you can check on him and what he is reading and share with him what you are reading or about to read from the bible. God can speak to him loud and clear from the bible, you should not underrate God's 'ability.' He can do all things. He is able to win anyone onto his side. Les is a good candidate to be used for God. Since he has agreed that I can talk to him, if I want, I will like to prepare you ahead of time that my next letter will be addressed to both of you. Let him also know that I will be interested in talking to him anytime you make a brief telephone call. I will be expecting your call, but make sure you do so whenever Les is around. Continue to be a little Christ to him. God loves you. He is working with you in Les' life. God bless you.

Dear Les & Bev,

It was nice to talk to both of you the other day. Les, you are a good guy, and easy to talk to. I hope both of you are still talking about God, even though Les say he doesn't really believe in him. Les, the good news is, God believes in you, He knows where you live, what you do and what you are up to. God loves all of you unconditionally.

As I was told, Bev did not make her stand known to you, Les, that she was a strong believer in Jesus Christ. And you, too, Les, did not make your disbelief in God known to Bev. Both of you took it for granted that it doesn't matter and that love supersedes religion. Yes, love is blind! You realized now that religion is a big issue, fighting about religion has ruined many marriages. I hope you will find something to do about it. No religion among many couples is even better than 50/50 – one believes and one doesn't. But it is good that your children have opted out of the game – going to Sunday school is no longer an issue. I hope you will keep it like that.

The question still remains, what do you need to do to solve the problem of religion between you? How are you going to handle the situation of the new religion that is trying to find its way into your home? I will like to suggest that you do what you neglected to do years ago while you were dating. Find time to talk about what is trying to separate you, and focus on what unites you. Both of you have to remember how you have been brought up. Religion is very important to your parents on both sides, especially the Christian faith. Les the existence of God was not a question until you got to university. Your parents had done their part with regards to passing Christianity on to you – which you embraced with joy, followed by Believer's Baptism.

As I suggested earlier, you need to have effective communication:

- You will need to ask yourselves, why and why not go to church?
- What wonders of God have we witnessed?
- What do we need from him?
- What are our expectations for our children?
- Can we survive without God?
- What is the importance of his words in our home?
- When all is said and done on earth, what's next?

All these questions and perhaps others would lead you to have a meaningful conversation. There is no winner or loser. A winning conversation is one that saves your marriage; the opposite will be anything that will have an adverse effect on your love for each other- anything that may want to put an end to your marriage. While you were dating, you trusted each other so much. Your love for each other was 100%. The question now is; what is the percentage of your love for each other? I don't want to leak the answer to that question. Just ask yourselves. Would you allow religion to snatch your lover from you? You need to handle the situation smartly.

Without an iota of doubt, God loves you, he trusts you. He was there when you were dating. Bev told me that she prayed a lot before she met you, and she believed that you are God's answer to her prayers. If possible, you may reflect on the early part of your lives and try to see God in your lives by then and strive to fill the vacuum in your marriage with him. He is the author of marriage and can make your marriage successful. You can never be a loser, if you believe in Jesus. Victory will be yours, if you can allow him into your marital life. Keep in touch.

Dear Les & Bev,

I really enjoyed our conversation on the phone last week. I am glad that you went away last month to talk and have fun together. Your focus that weekend was about the damage the religion issue is causing in your home. You have agreed to take some actions, Les, you have decided to stop your co-workers from coming to your house for religious rites. Since you have taken action on what you said, they have not come back to your home. Bev, you feel secure with Les' decision. Your children are also happy to know that your home is no longer a home for a foreign religion and that they can talk freely with their dad about what they have learned in Sunday school. They were even bold enough to ask you, Les, why you don't go with them to church.

You have accomplished a lot since my last letter. I understood that the children are aware that religion is causing trouble in your home. They know that you are one as a family during the week, but during the weekend you are two. The children are also happy that those guys have stopped coming to your house. Not that they don't like to receive visitors, but they don't want a strange religion in their home. Keep on doing a good job.

Perhaps it will be nice, if you can find time to tell them about different kinds of religions, as many as you know. You may try to identify each one with its beliefs. Lay emphasis on Christianity and what makes it unique – Christ was born in a special way; God's messenger from heaven (Angel Gabriel announced his conception to Mary, his mother, without any sexual intercourse with Joseph, his earthly father-the Holy Spirit entered into Mary's womb. A host of heavenly angels announced his birth by singing glory to God in the highest heaven and peace on earth on all whom God favor with the specific instructions of his birth to the Shepherd, who were keeping watch over their flock at night as to where he was to be found. Born to save the world from its sin (Matt. 1: 18-21, John 3:16). He lived a holy life; he died on the cross for humanity; he was buried and resurrected on the third day, he was the only religious leader who died and rose again; his resurrection gave his followers the assurance that they, too, will be resurrected one day (I Cor. 15:35-58); because of his resurrection, which was death's obituary-death was dead. It was defeated or swallowed up in a big victory (I Cor. 15:54). It would be great, if your children can know the rudiment of Christianity. Christ is the Son of God, and he and his Father, God, and the Holy Spirit – the third person in the God head – are one. Christians are not serving three Gods, but One. Jesus, his Father, and the Holy Spirit are one, which we call Trinity.

You should not listen to the devil's deception. He is the father of all liars. He lied to Adam and Eve years ago. Don't welcome his deceit. God is good, he is alive, and he is the Creator of the universe. Adam and Eve fell from God's plans for them, the devil wanted them to be like God, but instead they became unlike God (Gen.3).

Both of you ought to familiarize yourselves with the bible. It will be a good idea if you can find time to read and study the bible together, along with your children. The devil doesn't have anything good for you, but God does. God loves you both and your children. All of you are his children. He has no grandchildren. Everyone – old or young who confesses Jesus as his/her Savior becomes a child of God. The devil may be lying that God does not exist. Yes, he does exist! You are a living testimony of his existence. He created you in his image. Testify to that, and don't allow any religion to confuse you that God has no child or children. He does, Christ is his Son and you, I and others who believe in him are his children. Worship him together. He loves you. He is able to do all things for you. He is able to meet your needs and sustain your marriage. Pray to him. God bless you.

Dear Bev & Les,

Greetings to you all. I am delighted that you have been having family devotion every night with your children. You share the passage of the scripture you read together and you pray in turns every night. Wow! Les, that is marvelous and you have taken on the leadership role. Bev, you have been doing a good job. You are bringing the scripture stories to your kids' level, and making good use of your Sunday school teaching experience. You also go to mid-week bible study/prayer meeting. You're doing a great job. I am so thankful to God for both of you.

To authenticate your commitment to Christ, Les, I am wondering, if you could consider baptism. Or have you been baptized? Your children are old enough to decide on their own. Parents don't need to decide for their children – except in those denominations where they do infant baptism and confirmation service at a later stage. You need to check with them, if they are ready to commit their lives to Jesus Christ. If Les has been baptized, maybe what he needs to do is a re-commitment. You can discuss it with your pastor.

Now that you are both in Christ, I will like you to unite together in all ways. Do not let the enemy – Satan - deceive you, fight him always together on your knees. Tell him that you are in one camp and that you will no longer tolerate his lies. He is always afraid of anyone who prays. Try to always fill the gap between you. In other words, do not allow any space in between you. God has given you authority over the devil, and you have to use your authoritative tool – prayer – to reject his deceit. Stop buying his lies. He is the father of liars. He always fears anyone who prays. A prayer-less Christian is a power-less Christian. The more we pray, the more power is giving to us by Jesus. The less we pray, the less power we possess. The authenticity of prayer must be used over Satan.

Since you are now speaking the same language in regards to your faith in Jesus Christ, *the atmosphere in your home is different*. The devil almost put an end to your marriage. If there are some misunderstandings or offences between you, I will advise you to talk about it, humble yourselves, apologize to each other, and try to forgive each other. You have to forget about the past and focus on your future. Work as a team; try to put the devil under your feet, that is where he belongs. Focus on what unites you – your marriage, your children, your love and commitment to each other and God, the author of both your marriage and faith. The love of Christ binds you together now than before. Now, you love each other because Christ loves you unconditionally, and he wants you to do the same. God is able to help you continue loving each other unconditionally, too. Let this kind of agape - unconditional -love be your guide and transmit it to your children.

Let your flag of one faith, one family, and one God continue to fly. In unity there is strength and power. Don't allow division again. Be faithful to God; go to church and prayer meetings as you have been doing. I believe Jesus Christ will continue to honor himself by being faithful to his promises because of you. Be blessed in him.

Dear Les & Bev

Yes, you are right. It has been a while since we've been in touch with one another. Lots of water has passed under the Bridge since we spoke. Your children have been baptized and Les, you rededicated your life to God. That must have made Bev feel great! What about Mr. and Mrs. James – Les' parents? That must have been one of the things that they have been waiting for. Well, congratulations to all of you. Your prayer life is going on well. Your understanding of the scripture is increasing daily. I am delighted to hear such things.

So what's next for you in your Christian journey? I am sure there are many "old" Les and Bev around today who are fighting for or even that have lost their marriages. What can you do to help them? I will hope that the "new" Les and Bev would like to share their experiences with others. Whoever you can help would become your neighbors in faith. Religion issue between couples should not be taken lightly. There are two categories of people you can help. One, the intended couples. Those that are seriously dating but their love is blind – they have the opinion that "little issue" like religion does not matter. They are thinking that they would be able to handle it without any problems – remember you have been there. After "I do" they will realize that it is one of the major issues in marital life. If you can find a way to help young people who are dating that will be great. You have to tell them about your story. You will need to help them to be open to each other, to ask questions and not to take anything for granted. The dating couple may think that it is okay to neglect religion while dating, but as their marital journey begins and goes on, they will notice that it can easily boost their love for and commitment to each other and at the same time, lack of it can easily doom their marriage. It will be great, by God's help, if you can do your best to help aspiring couples.

In my judgment, the second category of people you can partner with in rescuing marriage are the marital couples who are in a big mess because of uncompromised faith. There are many husbands and wives out there without peace because A goes to church or believes in God, while B is the opposite. You may quickly guess what that may be. If you know any couple like that, you can prayerfully consider helping them out. We were saved to lead others to the Savior. God is looking for many laborers to work in the field. God will be honored, I believe, if you can volunteer to help troubled marital couples facing religious issues.

You can start a small group or a group, perhaps in your church or in your community to facilitate discussions on how to reach a compromise on this issue, otherwise, many husbands and wives will continue to have problems. Someone has to be there for them to help safe their marriage from reaching a disastrous end. If you or I don't want to help out, who will? Do whatever you can to be a blessing to others as God has blessed you in saving your marriage.

If you decide to help others to save their prospective marriages or existing ones, you have to be careful not to over work yourselves. As you will be trying to help others, you have to plan how to continue to care for your marriage as well as yourselves and your children. I believe God will continue to strengthen your marriage. Seek his face daily and do your best to please him. It has been a great opportunity for me to be involved in your lives for the past years. I thank God for you and hope to see more of God in your home.

Chapter 12
Peter and Joy - Second Marriage

Dear Joy and Peter,

I enjoyed our telephone conversation the other day. It is nice to know, as you mentioned during the phone call that you have been to my website.

You have both been married before, but your first marriages did not work out. And as of now, you are wondering what will happen to your current marriage. You knew each other from work, even though you said you were not that close until both of you were divorced. I am wondering how bitter and hurtful your separation and divorce processes were? If both of you did not have friendly settlements with your former partners, I'm wondering if there is any trace of anger or frustration or bitterness in both of you toward your exes. If this is the case, each one of you may likely be a scapegoat. In fact, the divorce rate for second marriages is higher than the rate for first marriages. But do not be discouraged, you can save your marriage, if you want to!

As I mentioned earlier, if there is anger somewhere toward your exes, you have to let go of that, in order for you to have a meaningful relationship in your new marriage. It would be too painful to undergo another heartache. Try to forgive each other. And perhaps you have to stop talking negatively about your former relationships – unless, if it's with thanksgiving. That is try to thank each other by saying "I never received this kind of honor or high rating from my former...I didn't even know what love was all about in my former marriage"...Thank you Joy/Peter for being such a loving, caring and supportive wife/husband." Positive comparison is okay – with attitude of appreciation toward each other. However, negative comparisons like the following are not good: "Even though my Ex was not a loving, caring husband/wife, but he/she was always patient with me." "My former husband/wife was always home from work on time. I wonder why you are always late from work." These kind of negative comments are not helpful in any healthy second marriage. If you are currently in this situation, you need to refrain from it. Try to be positive and talk directly to each other, no comparisons.

You need to let go of your ex, though it has been about four/five years since you left your former partners, and about two years since you have been in this new relationship. Old plus new are not a good match. Forgive your exes because of your new marriage and also because of your own well-being. Anger is not good for you. Don't poison your liver. Let go, let God. Try to start a new life. Time of fighting is supposed to be over when each one of you said it was over with your former partners. See each other as the one you will spend the rest of your life with. When you exchanged vows, you said: "I do." I do means; "I will" not "I may." Let your yes – I will – continue to be so. I believe you like each other as you demonstrated love to and care for each other before you went to the altar to say I do. Let the candle of your love, care, likeness continue burning. I will encourage you to start praying together and praying for each other, if you have not been doing so. Study the bible together. Let me know how you are getting along. May the God of peace give you peace.

Dear Joy & Peter,

I got your letter a couple of days ago. Thank you for your honesty. You admitted that you were still angry with your exes. You talked it over between yourselves. As you have said, you agreed to let go of the past. I am glad to hear that. You have done yourselves and your marriage a big favor by forgiving your former husband/wife. They may not know that you did, but you know and your new relationship will know it also.

It seems that many things went wrong with your former relationships, and things are threatening to also go wrong with your new relationship. It is obvious that you are too busy and your busy lives are affecting your communication. It is good to be busy, but you need time for each other as well as for your individual self. Text messages telephone calls, and emails cannot replace face-to-face marital communication. I am talking about effective communication. As you are obliged to your jobs, you should also be to your marriage. God brought you together at this time for a purpose. Do not blame yourself for the death of your former marriages. Learn something from it, and try to correct your own faults. If I may say, I would like each of you to write down the reasons why the former marriages ended. This is not time to blame him or her. It is time to be honest individually and with each other. Find a good weekend to do this exercise.

Talk about it. Pray to God to help you admit your faults. Talk about both of your weaknesses. No judgment, no condemnation, no, "wow! is that you? You did that?" It is supposed to be a time to learn, a time to bring something beautiful out of something ugly. The questions you should be asking at the end of the exercise should be: "How can I avoid making similar mistakes, and change my bad attitude?" Be sincere with each other and to yourself, personally. Doing this exercise is not to talk about the weak sides of the exes, but to find out how you can help your new marriage. If possible, write down what you need to change, what needs to be corrected, what needs to be improved and you should address the questions, how can I be a better husband/wife this time around? What can we learn from our mistakes? There is no Mr. or Mrs. Perfect in any failed marital relationship. Both couples shared in the failure.

If the exercise is done well, it is not only going to help you to know each other better or to admit your faults. It will improve your communication. Talk with each other with sincerity without any assumptions. Talk loud and clear. While you are talking with each other, do not hesitate to ask questions. It is better to clarify things than to assume from what he/she says. Also do not assume that she/he should know, because you know.

The more you find time to talk, the more you will know each other better. The more you know each other, the more likely you will appreciate or accept each other. The more you do that, the more you will fall in love, that is, the greater your love and care for each other. The little fights you have been having will quickly disappear, if you can sincerely find time to communicate effectively. Try it and let me know, if there is progress. God bless you

Dear Peter & Joy,

I am so happy that you had a good getaway weekend and that you were also able to talk about the past. Your last marriages were not successful just because you and your former wife/husband did not find time to iron things out. Some of the killers of your past marriages, according to you, were: My right, financial issues; sexual intercourse; lack of effective communication; lack of commitment and uncompromising love. Thank God that you were able to recognize all of these. Since you know your enemies, I hope you will try to run away from them.

You want me to address some of these marriage killers. "My right," Some couples don't mind the consequence of their anger. They would do their best to fight for their rights, to make sure that they win the argument. Many of them won their discussions or arguments but they lost their marriages. "My right," this is not to say that one doesn't need to know his/her right, but to put others in his/her own shoes. People should think about the possible outcome of what they are doing. When you are discussing, try not to turn it into an argument. There is no winner or loser in a marriage communication. Have each other in mind whenever you are talking. What you will not want your partner to do to you, don't do it to him/her.

Your marriage brought you together and you have to have it in mind. The more you demonstrate concern for your marriage, the more you will like to save it. Don't be a winner or a loser when you are communicating, but be a saver of your marriage. Many couples don't like to stop first when they are expressing anger. One must be a sheep. Sheep are kind, gentle animals. Try to take it easy when A offends B. Be cool and calm. This is not a matter of being stupid, but rather about being smart to save your marriage and wise enough not to upset your partner. Whenever we are angry or try to fight for our rights, we don't always consider the outcome of the lashing words. Ask yourself a question whenever "my right" comes to mind – where is my marriage's right? Remember, when you said I do, you were also indirectly saying, "I do believe, I can save my marriage, I can be my husband's/wife's keeper, I can be a helper, I can be his/her comforter, I can be his/her lover, I can be a good friend to him/her, and I can be a good wife/husband to him/her."

When you care about saving your marriage, you will commit yourself to it. At work, you always want to be a good worker, perhaps you do that in order to be promoted and not to lose your job. The same commitment you have to please your bosses at work should also be present in your marriage. Try to please your partner not as your boss, but as someone who needs your love, care, support, and friendship. Have God's "right" to institute marriage in mind and let it support your "right." I believe you can make it and you *will* make it. It is high time to bring your marriage back to its Author- use your God's lifetime warranty before it's too late. God loves you and your marriage, and so do I. Pray always.

Dear Peter & Joy,

I read your letter with joy and I appreciate your nice comments. Thank you. I know what it means to let go of one's right for the sake of peace, oneness and love in marriage. Keep up the good job. Feel free to educate your married friends that they sometimes need to do the same thing. That will make them smart at the end of the day.

In your letter, you mentioned that you would like me to talk about love and romantic love. You both agreed that your sexual intercourse was not good in your previous marriages, for the fact that your love for each other by then was not genuine. Peter, your mom left home for another man, when you were five. Your mother's love was not there for you. Thank God for your Dad, who raised you by himself, he did his best. Your mom also did what she thought was right for her at the time. It is now your turn to do what you can to love yourself as well as your wife. Paul the apostle advised husbands to love their wives as Christ loved the church and gave his life for her. Paul wants husbands to love their wives as their own bodies. "...He who loves his wife loves himself. After all, no one ever hated his own body, but he feeds and cares for it, just as Christ does the church" (Eph. 5:28-29) (NIV). Paul concluded that chapter by saying "However, each one of you also must love his wife as he loves himself, and the wife must respect her husband" (v.33) (NIV). Both of you must exchange love for each other

The love Jesus Christ demonstrated toward us is an agape type of love. God's love to us is unconditional. He wants you to love each other unconditionally. When genuine love is present in marriage, many good things will follow. Sexual intercourse will not be meaningful or done with sincerity when the true love is not there. For you to enjoy yourselves sexually, you must first love each other. Sex will come easily when love is ruling in a marital relationship. Do not have sex just to have sex, but to enjoy it. Sex is one of the biggest items in God's marriage package to humanity. Sex promotes love and love helps sex to be enjoyable. Love and sex are con-joined. They go hand-in-hand, so you have to love each other and care for each other. Share your bed and your bodies to have a good relationship.

God cares for you and your marriage. He knows divorce hurts, it is a killer – many divorcees have killed themselves, physically, emotionally, mentally and spiritually. As God loves you, you ought to love each other. I Corinthians 13:4-8 show us a test of love. The apostle Paul writes about what love is and what it's not. Love is patient – love never fails ---. I like it to be read like this – let your name replace love, for example, Peter is patient, Joy is kind, Peter is not self- seeking, Joy does not boast, and so on. Write it out and read it aloud to each other. Feel free without judgment to remind each other when one of you behaves contrary to any of the sayings. Test yourselves and let your shortcomings be the area each one of you should work on. Pray for real love from God for each other. God bless you.

Dear Joy & Peter,

Two cannot walk together unless they have agreed to do so (Amos 3:3). It is good to know that you are doing things together better than before. It is also nice to know that you are communicating better. You have improved your ability to listen and ask questions, if you are unsure of what the other is trying to say. Good for you. Yes, when you stop fighting, you will be able to talk more in love. The more you love each other, the more your relationship will improve. Try to stop carry over anger and bitterness from your previous marriages or relationships. We need to let go and let God, that is, let God be in charge of the situations about your past, present, and your future.

I am very positive that you will continue to fall in love daily and to date each other as you did before you got married. Your marriage is a life contract. The "I do" you said at your wedding meant "I will," not "I may" and it is for life. The good news is that there is a "lifetime warranty" for your marriage. If you buy anything in the store and it has a lifetime warranty, if you have any problems with it, what would you do? I will imagine you will take it back to the store, perhaps with your receipt. Similarly, you have a lifetime warranty on your marriage. The principal of the marriage institute, God, is still there. He is the author of marriage. He knows how to fix any broken or almost broken marriages. He is the unchangeable Changer. Nothing is impossible with him. He wants us to come to him, through Jesus Christ, if we have any problems or burdens. Jesus himself said: "Come to me, all you who are weary and burdened, and I will give you rest. Take my yoke upon you and learn from me, for I am gentle, and humble in heart, and you will find rest for your souls. For my yoke is easy and my burden is light" (Matt 11:28) (NIV).

It will be easier to take broken or almost broken marriages to the One, God, who established it. Do not wait until your marriage is totally broken, that is, uncontrollable fights or separation or even divorce, before you go to God, Mr. Marriage fixer. Tell him anytime you have a small fight or misunderstanding or are in an unpleasant situation, he knows what to do to *straighten* things up for you. In fact, you don't need to wait until troubled times before you talk to him. Pray to him daily, study the word of God together. If you start your day with God together, you will not end it with bitterness or anger against each other. People say the couple that stays together prays together. But I prefer it this way – the couple that prays together stays together. My friends, more prayers mean more happiness, joy, peace, love, etc., but it is the opposite with less prayers. A Christian couple should focus on God with regards to their marriage. God who instituted marriage knows what to do to make it work. Depend on him not only for your marriage, but for all aspects of your lives. He loves you and he cares for you and your marriage. He will not leave you nor forsake you. Remember, there is a life warranty on your marriage from God. Be blessed in the Lord always.

Dear Peter & Joy,

It's wonderful to know that you had a great 5th anniversary celebration! You went away for one week. Wow, second honeymoon!! I am also happy to know that you have started to enjoy marriage now. As you mentioned in your memo to me, this is the first time in your marriage that you are seeing yourselves as a wife/husband. As you have said, you carried the baggage of "I am not a good enough wife/husband" into your new relationship. Since your exes used to say negative things about you, you believed the things and carried the negativity, into your new marriage. I thank God that you have rejected those negative comments. You have started to see good things in yourselves as an individual and you know that you are wonderfully created by God. Let negative feelings toward yourself, each other, your marriage and life in general be put to rest. Let them die and be buried forever.

It will be a good idea to let your friends; married ones in particular, know how you are now feeling in comparison to how you used to feel about yourselves and your old marriages. What you say is what you get. Negative plus negative will always be a big failure, with the exception of mathematics where negative plus negative is always positive. Try to educate your friends to be positive about their lives and marriages. Of course, positive plus positive should be a good success. To have a successful life and a good marriage, one has to say something good about him/herself. You don't need to give the devil any grounds to stand with regard to your lives or marriage. So Peter and Joy, continue to profess good things about yourselves and your marriage. The Holy Spirit or the Angel of the Lord will make it happen for you. Remember again, what you say is what you get. God wants the best for you. He has good thoughts toward your marriage. When you are positive about your marriage, you are inviting God to breathe the breath of life into it. I believe you know that God is able to make the dry bones live again. Ezekiel the prophet was told to prophesy to the dry bones. He did and the breath of God entered into the dry bones (Ezekiel 37:1-14). The bones came to life, any dying marriage, even a dead one, can come to life by the breath of God. Call on God always to breathe on your marriage and on each one of you, too. Our God is the same yesterday, today and forever (Heb. 13:8). He is able to do all things and to perfect everything that concerns you. He is able to keep whatever you entrusted into his hands.

I am positive that you will continue to excel in your marriage. Don't be tired of doing good to each other. Try to be a good example to the couples around you. Pray and study the words of God together, and of course, do not neglect fellowship with others (Heb. 10:25). And the God of peace, hope, love and joy will continue to be with you, uphold you and your marriage. His grace is sufficient for you.

Chapter 13
James and Julia – Second Marriage with a Troubled Step-Son

Dear James & Julia

I was thrilled when I heard that you knew Amy & Brad. I also enjoyed our conversation the other day. You mentioned that this is James's first marriage and Julia's second. Julia, your marriage came to an end after 5years, and you have a three-year-old boy. James is not pleased with your son's attitude around the home. Your son, Jason, always drives James nuts. This has caused a big tension between you. You don't have enough time for each other. Your relationship is shaken after six months of marriage.

I believe that you both loved and liked each other before you said I do. You also knew that Julia had Jason in her life. James, I know it is a new thing for you. You've never been married and all of a sudden, you have taken on the double role of a husband and father. James, what would you do, if Jason is your biological son? Jason thinks he is having fun. You can act as a model to correct him in love and to educate him on how to behave. You and Julia need to agree together on how to train Jason. To Julia, Jason is a kid. He needs to be a kid. Julia said both of you need patience and understanding. Yes, it is true. You both need to be patient with Jason and to understand that he is alone, and has nobody else to play with. He thinks he needs his mom all the time. Both James and Jason are perhaps jealous of each other and Julia you are stuck in between. You are trying to balance your role as a wife and mom.

I would like to suggest to you, James, to see Jason as your own son – I am not saying that you should replace Jason's dad, but that you should be there for Jason. Jason also has some adjustments to make. Unless Jason has abnormal behavior – if he does, I will recommend that you go and see a doctor, let Jason be Jason, let him be a kid. Correct him together when necessary, praise him when need be. James, remember that you love Julia and that was the reason you married her. Your love for Julia should reflect in Jason by the way you care for him.

Julia, I can sense that you love Jason dearly and you want the best for him. You left his dad because things were not going well for both of you. I am wondering how Jason is reacting to a different man trying to be "Dad" to him. Is there any indication that he resents James through his behavior at home? Each one of them is taking a big role in your life. Take it easy. Things will get better as time goes on. Both of you have a long way to go, but I will be there for you, and God is able to give you peace and wisdom to deal with the situation.

Dear James & Julia,

I am glad to know that you have been adjusting to the situation at home. By the way, I do appreciate your comments. Jason is almost four, his dad just moved to a city further away. I believe that Jason understands that.

James, it is nice that you are trying to accept Jason more and more. You have been taken him out to the park by yourself-without his mom. This is very good of you. A joke for you James- are you jealous of Jason's dad any time he comes to pick-up or drop off Jason every other weekend? Well, he is far away now. He is no more around to look at your beautiful wife's (Julia) face. So you are taking it easy. Good to know!!! On a serious note, you both need some adjustments. James, you should not be too overwhelmed by a double role – as a husband and "dad." Julia, your ex was not there for you, he was a workaholic and at the same time, you lived by yourself one year before James came into your life. James has never been married. James needs to know that he is no longer alone. James, you cannot do things as you used to, you have someone to talk with, to seek advice from and share your opinion with. You also have someone to father. You need Godly wisdom to balance your roles as a husband, "father" and manager at your workplace. Try to relax, hang your frustrations at work, if there is any, on the doorpost of your office when you are coming home. Try to perform your duty at home, which is different from office management, even though God put your family in your charge to care for, and manage with your better half. Life must be different from the single life you have been used to. You must find means to know how to play your double role at home. You need to be there for Jason and to fall in love with Julia all the time. Don't try to see Jason as a hindrance to your love for his mom or his mom to yours.

Julia ought to let go of the-"I know how, I've been doing it for about three years, I know better" attitudes-prior marital experience and parenting. Remember, two are better than one. And two can only walk together if they agree (Amos 3:3). Try to carry James along with you, even in regards to Jason's matters. God put James on your way to help you raise Jason and to share things together. it is not only a man that is not good to be alone, I guess it is also not good for a woman to be alone – if I am wrong, you can correct me – that was the reason why God joined you together. When you are fighting, is that not saying to God, guess what, God, you are wrong? God is always right, he never makes any mistakes. For both of you, James and Julia, to be together in marriage, it is God's doing. Try to appreciate his plan for your life. God knows it can work. Don't prove him wrong. Forget about the past. Start a new life, plan together, talk, support each other, appreciate each other, and care for each other; all these will promote your love for each other and create a healthy home for Jason and his brother and sister to come, right? Keep in touch God bless you.

Dear Julia & James,

Many good things have been happening. You have celebrated your first anniversary, Jason turned four, James you turned 34 and Julia 31. You must have been busy for the past two months? Did you buy a restaurant for the merry making? I am just joking. I am happy to say congratulations to the three of you. You are all one year older. Your love for each other must be stronger, too!

You want me to talk more about communication. You are right to say that communication is one of the killers and savers in marriage. When using it effectively, it promotes love, better understanding, care, and increases trust. But if communication is not done effectively, it can do a lot of damage in a marriage. I will advise that you to find time out of no time to communicate effectively with each other. Feel free to ask questions when necessary, and do not assume you know what A or B is saying. Do not reach a conclusion based on your own imagination. Do not assume. Assumptions can easily kill communication. What you think A means may not be what he/she meant. Communicate loud and clear. It's not good to argue, but to talk. You need to understand each other, to reach a conclusion whenever you are talking, and if you don't have the time to reach a conclusion, you can defer it till you have the time. Jason should not be the focus of your attention or major topic of your communication. You need to share each other's work load. You should help lessen each other's burdens from your workplaces.

You also need to talk and plan for children of your own. You said you want a boy and a girl. You ought to talk about planning for them. It will be a smart idea, whenever you communicate with each other to pay full attention. Do not allow anything to be in between you; no radio, television, or computer on; no distractions, 100% concentration. God always communicates with us loud and clear. Try your best to be like him. Be serious, but don't be too serious. I would like to suggest to you to include God in your communication. Start to have a good communication *with* him and allow him to do the same with you through his words. Learn from him. Talk to him together each day. It will be a good idea to start your day and to end it with God. When you start the day with God, you will not fight each other during the day as long as you determine to watch out. God loves you and he is interested in you and your marital life. He established marriage. When things are wrong, he knows what to do. He is very smart to fix marriages without traces of the knots. Don't hesitate to bring your troubles to God as a means of using your marital lifetime warranty. May he help you in your marital communication and listen to you all the time.

Dear James & Julia,

It is good to know that your communication has been improving and that Jason is doing much better, he is relaxing more and is much friendlier *with* James. I hope things will continue to be better and better for you.

You wanted me to write to you about love. According to what I have gathered from you, you are far better than where you were about a year ago. As long as you are trying to improve yourself, you are doing something and you will get there, slowly but surely. Love is a big fundamental aspect of a good marriage. When love is missing, marriage is dying or even dead. The greater the marital love, the more happiness and joy in any couple's home. Love is the glue that *sticks* a marriage together. There are different kinds of love: romantic love, friendly love and most importantly, unconditional love. Love in any marriage supposed to be unconditional. If you love somebody for superficial reasons, when the reason is gone, the love may likely go, too. But agape love – unconditional love, the kind of love God has for the world (John 3:16) is what you need to have for each other. God loves you unconditionally, and you ought to do so for each other.

When unconditional love is there, the other kind of love will follow. Let's briefly talk about romantic or sexual love. When you love your spouse, of course, you will like to give your body to him/her. Neither husband nor wife needs to beg or treat the other; mutual understanding and readiness to have a good time should be the ultimate goals. Buy gifts for each other on special occasions and other moments you feel like giving. Many husbands like to bring flowers home for their wives to surprise them and to let them know that they are loved. This is great, but agape kind of love is more than flowers or kissing all the time. Do not get me wrong, I am not saying James should not be doing that or should stop doing it – but all I am saying is that a genuine love is not all about that, but it includes *all* of them. Many couples love themselves so much and since you are part of each other's life, it means loving each other is- loving yourself. Therefore, James, do yourself a favour- love Julia. Julia, do something great for yourself-love James. When A upsets B, the one who causes the pain may be upset, too. For you not to upset yourself, don't upset each other.

All the good things you want for yourself, Julia, you need to wish it for James and vice versa. Talk together at home with happiness and joy and it will give a sense of security to Jason and your baby on the way. It will be obvious to them that you love each other. They will take the fruits of the love you plant in your home to anywhere they go. The book of Songs of Solomon in the bible and (I Cor.13) are good to read often. Don't stop falling in love, communicate effectively and remember your commitment.

May the God of peace grant you joy, peace, patience, and all good things. Keep fit in the Lord. Keep in touch. God bless.

Chapter 14
Dave and Deb – Blended Marriage/Family

Dear Dave & Deb,

It was nice to meet you at the park. I enjoyed our conversation on the phone, too. How are your children? As you said, Dave has three children from his previous marriage and Deb has two. Deb's children are living with you, while Dave's children are living with their mom about 10 minute-drive from your home. Dave, Deb said that each time you go to pick up or drop off your children, you always spend a lot of time before coming home. Consequently, she is wondering if you are still talking with your ex. She also said that she read some text messages from your ex that seem to indicate that you still have some feelings for her. In addition, she noted that you always buy expensive things for your children. However, you are trying to say Deb is incorrect.

Deb, I would like to commend your efforts in narrating these things to me. But I am wondering if your ex is faithful to your own children with regards to spending time with them, anytime he comes to see them. He is far away from your city. I also wonder if he has been given money to or spending money on your two children. Deb, is your ex faithful financially to you or your children, could it be because you are still fighting or because he does not have a good job? If you are not ready to let go of your past with your ex, it is not going to help you in this relationship. You need to try to forgive your ex. Try to talk to him to be faithful in giving custody expenses, and perhaps you have to report him to the authorities through your lawyer, so that he can play his own part in raising your children. You need peace, so does your ex as well. Try to settle things with your ex and strive to involve Dave more in raising your kids. I am not trying to say that you are jealous of Dave's ex, but if an element of jealousy is there, that will not take your marriage anywhere, except trouble. You and Dave need to find time to talk and try to understand each other and establish trust.

Dave, it is good that you are spending good quality time with your own children. I am wondering if you are there for Deb's kids. If you have not been spending good quality time with them, I will advise that you start to do so right away. Both of you know that you have children with your exes, and for the past year that you have married, there was no real peace not only because of the kids, but for some other issues as well. You need to wear big shoes in this case, Dave. The father of Deb's children lives far away and he can't see his children every other week as you see yours. You should find time to talk about how to blend your kids together. Let Deb's children and even Deb go with you whenever you want to drop off your kids. Since you have a seven passenger van, why not? Give peace a chance; you don't need to fight on little stuff like that. Allow Deb to trust you. You have already said no to your ex and since you have said "yes, I do" to Deb, you have to honour your vows. Try to be there for her with regards to raising her children. It is good that you and your ex are still friends; you can bring your new wife, Deb into your friendship. I know many couples like that. Talk to Deb about it, and even shop together for all the kids, not just yours. Keep in touch. I will love to do so with you, too. God bless you.

Dear Dave & Deb,

It's great that you've started to communicate effectively together regarding your five kids. For Easter, you said you shopped together for them. That is so good of you. Dave, it is nice that Deb's children went with you a couple of times when you went to pick up and drop off your children. That's good that you're trying to develop a friendship between them.

You mentioned that you are still having some issues with your finances. You are both blessed with good jobs, and you don't have to drive too far to your workplaces. The inability to control finance was one of the issues in Deb's former relationship. You ought to talk and plan your finances. You are living in Dave's house which is almost paid off. Do you have a common purse or pay 50/50 toward your house keeping or have you decided who pays for what? Whatever method you are using you have to talk and plan together. It would be nice, if A can know before B buys expensive items. If the idea of shopping together or planning for what you need and when to buy can be incorporated into your system, it can be helpful for you. By the way, do you have a budget – monthly or yearly – or you just spent your money as need be?

In fact, money is one of the biggest marriage killers. Plan your spending well, how much to spend on your five children, on your four parents, house-keeping and other things. Let A know what B is doing. Paying bills may be frustrating sometimes. Remember, what God has joined together, financial issues should not put asunder. Do not let money cause problems between you, but let it unite you. You are blessed to have it, be a good "manager" of your money. I know you both deserve good cars, how many thousands of dollars you spend on cars is not the issue here, but rather your agreement on which kind of cars you need and how much you want to spend should be the focus. Just talk and try to agree on who drives which car and how many vehicles you want to own. If all seven of you have to travel or go somewhere, you need a 7 passenger vehicle. A car will be okay, if you need to go to work or go out locally with one person or less than six any car will be fine. All you need is effective communication.

God wants the best for you. You are blessed to afford the best, but it would be wise to involve God in your spending. Let God have a say in every aspect of your lives, talk to him and ask him what to buy and how to spend your money. We are all caretakers of what we have. God entrusted all we have into our hands with the hope that we will use what we have or who we are to glorify his name. Whatever you have, let God's glory be seen in it. God loves you. He blessed you with five beautiful children and with so many resources. Be appreciative of all you have and let them promote your love and marital relationship. May you be blessed more by the Lord.

Dear Deb & Dave,

You have decided to go for common purse. You have to decide how you will be spending every cent of your both incomes. I wish you all the best. The issue before you now is in-laws. You are both blessed to have all your four parents alive in their 70s. Deb's parents are in your city, Dave, your parents are four-hour drive away. Whenever they visit, they always like to spend a couple of days with you. Sometimes they pass negative comments on Deb's children. She is not happy at times with such.

I've started to think about how Dave's parent are somehow critical of your being together and it seems that Deb's parent are not ready to come to terms with their daughter's new blended family. Perhaps both of you have to decide what to tell your parents. They need to give you a chance to manage your family, otherwise, they may likely cause problems for you down the road. They are still thinking you are their babies, the same ones they knew forty years ago. But gone are those days. You are now a man/woman of your own family. Maybe each of you has to speak to your parents personally in the language they will understand. Let them know that nobody can take their place in your lives and you will encourage them to see your husband/wife in you and your stepchildren as if they were your own children. Let them know that they are free to advise you, but not to criticize your husband/wife, if he/she offends them or they don't like what he/she does, they should let you know. Life fifty years ago is not the same today.

Am I assuming too much to say perhaps your parents on both sides are missing your exes or did they play a negative role in your former marriages? Whatever the case, let them know that you love your husband/wife and that both of you will do whatever you can for them as their children and that they should try to treat their step grandchildren well as they will treat their biological grandchildren. Try to educate the children to respect all their grandparents, and you both must do the same. Give them money or whatever their needs are. Treat them well, don't give room for any doubt in their mind that their son/daughter in-law loves them and cares for them. Treat your in-laws how you would like your in-laws to treat you. Above all, remember them in your prayers. Do whatever both of you can on their birthdays, anniversaries, and all special occasions; this is the time for them to enjoy the works of their hands – their labors in your upbringing. Let the love of Christ be seen in your home all the time. I will be praying for you.

Dear Dave & Deb,

It's good that you both had meetings with your parents. It is encouraging to know that they have taken what you discussed with them joyfully. I hope the tension between the two of you in regard to in-laws will die down. I believe you will continue to do your part and let them know that you are there for them.

You want me to talk about commitment. I am happy to know that you are both liked at work, your bosses and co-workers like you. They all acknowledge your commitment and that you're hard working. Dave, you were recently promoted as a director. By the way, I would like to say congratulations again. You have both committed a lot of your time, your energy and yourself-to your work. Great! You are investing a lot into your work to make everything super, and you're reaping the fruits. It would be good, if you can apply the same idea of commitment at work to your marriage. At work, you are always punctual, work diligently, and are nice to everyone. You can use the same principles in your marriage. Do things on time. Be nice to each other and your children. Work hard to please yourself and each other. Give peace a chance. Be honest and kind to each other.

When you exchanged your marriage vows about four years ago, promises were made before God and many people. You declared to be nice to each other, to love, to cherish and to be faithful. The "I do" you said meant "I will" not "I may." As you both have impressed your bosses to continually promote you, strive to impress each other for your marital promotion. The more you do your best to love, care and support each other, the more you are promoting the stability of your marriage.

As Christian couples, we should not be tired of giving and giving according to our marital vows, it is till death do us part. So your job is to commit yourselves to each other and to be faithful to that commitment. Many couples failed to honor their marital commitment and they have buried their marriages. In your case, God wants your marriage to be forever. I believe it is possible. Try to be faithful and remember your commitments to each other while dating. Keep the flag of commitment flying, may God continue to help you on your marital journey.

Dear Deb & Dave,

It was nice to talk to you on the telephone the other day. I promised to write you a letter so that you can refresh your memory. Since you don't tape our conversations, I know it may not be possible to remember everything. I understand that there are more demands on Dave from work. That is the nature of management. You have to fly to different countries and attend meetings here and there.

Dave, it is very kind of you that you always bring something special for your wonderful wife. You have been doing your best in that regard. Yet, Deb is still complaining. To her, she wants to have her husband at home and in bed more often. You fly out of the country 2 or 3 times a month and each trip takes you up to five days. Dave, do you still enjoy flying like that and when is it going to end? What I mean is; will there be any changes? Perhaps if you are obliged to be travelling so often, you should let Deb go with you occasionally. Deb can get some time off from work, maybe like two or three times a year. Additionally, it will be better to avoid unnecessary meetings or long meetings that will make you come home from work late practically every day. It is nice that you are a "big boss" at work and that a lot of money is coming home, but Deb is not happier than when you were in your former position with a lower salary.

Your job is very important and it is good to have a fat salary, but your marriage and your family are very important, too. Money cannot replace you at home. You have to be aware of signs of problems or crisis. In second marriage, divorce is more painful than the first one for some. Both of you ought to talk and understand each other. You need to make good use of the time you have whenever you're together. Dave, I hope that you do not bring work home. Your wife and children need more than your physical presence at home, interaction and involvement are necessary.

Deb, you have been doing a good job picking up Dave's children, whenever he cannot do so. I have to commend your efforts for keeping his children over the weekend whenever it is his turn. The most important thing both of you need is understanding and perhaps adjustment! You need to communicate and agree about what you should do or need to do. Above all, I will recommend to you to find time to seek God's face to help you to know what is to be done. He is able to enable you to love each other better than before. Study the words of God together. Allow the Holy Spirit to teach you what to do. If God can be in the center of your marriage, he will give you joy, peace, hope and he will increase your love and commitment for each other. Give him a place in your marriage. Let Jesus always be an unseen guest. He knows what to do to save your marriage. By doing the preceding, you're making use of God's lifetime warranty in your marriage. I am praying for more of his blessings on you, your family and your marriage. Keep in touch.

Chapter 15
Joe and Abby – Angry at God for infertility

Dear Joe,

This letter is to fulfill my promise. It was almost a week ago that I had the opportunity to talk with you when I visited your parents. As you know, your parents and I have known one another for the past 5 years. As I assured your parents and you that I will be talking to you, and I am happy that you, too, agreed.

As you said, you have been drinking for the past three or four years and use drugs occasionally. You have been having girl friends since you were in grade 7. You had more than 6 girls in total, one at a time. Your marks are not good enough. As of now, you are half way through grade 11. Joe, I want to remind you what I said to you; it is never too late to turn things around. I believe you said that you would like to be a lawyer. It is good that you have a big dream. You know what you want to be. To be a lawyer, you have to be more serious and focused. You yourself agreed that you should change your friends. Yes, you need to do so. Paul Apostle urges: "Bad company corrupts good character" (1Cor.15:33) (NIV). You need to stand by your word. Waiting for your last year in high school to be serious may likely be too late. You can bring up your marks now. If that can happen, it will help you in grade 12. Find yourself good and serious friends. Drugs are not good for you as well as too much drinking. It may be impossible for you to stop bad habits if you don't change your ways of doing things. You don't really need to have many friends, some good friends you have are more than enough as of now. As time goes on, you will be able to pick up more good and serious friends. It's okay to have an industrious girlfriend. In order for you to achieve your goal, you will need encouragers as your friends.

I believe you meant what you said, you want to turn your ways of doing things around. May I suggest that you have an appointment with your guidance counsellor in your school for course selections for grade 12. Share your dream with him or her. There is still hope for you to have good marks in grade 12, even in grade 11. Maintain a closer relationship with your parents. You should know that they both love and care for you. They are more than ready to help you to be what you want to be, and what God wants you to be. But remember, the only person who can change you is yourself. Indeed God has power to change you, but he needs your cooperation, and perhaps your permission to do so. Permission I meant is, God will not force anything on you or anyone. If you know you cannot do it on your own, you will need to humble yourself and seek help – from your parents, school and good friends, above all from God. God is always waiting for anyone to call on him for help. Since you are tired of your life style, you definitely need God in Jesus Christ to help you. Don't wait too long. There is a time for everything. I will be looking forward to hearing from you soon. Find time to pray, study hard and smart. May God show you his mercy, be gracious to you, and bless you with all good things. Amen.

Dear Joe,

Good stuff. I was so delighted to hear what you have been able to do since you got my letter. Your phone call made my day. You have spoken to your school guidance counsellor and you are praying with your parents about your future. You have dumped all your drinking buddies, and you have not been using drugs since last month. Good job. You have started to study hard and did well on your mid-terms. Excellent!

The new friends who have been helping you recover from drinking and drug use are now your project partners. You have been studying together and attending youth group meetings in their church. Your life style has changed. You don't have a girl-friend now. You also realized how many hours you have wasted on the phone, internet, texting etc. To be late is better than never. In a few weeks you have to finish this academic year, which is crucial. Since you have been doing well in your tests, projects, and also on your mid-term exams, I have confidence that you will have a good result at the end of your grade 11. Keep the flag flying. You can do it, yes you can! Just make sure you continue pressing on until you get what you want.

You asked me if you can be talking to your old drinking buddies about how and why you have changed your lifestyle. Why not, Joe? I believe it will be a good opportunity for you to share your story as well as your dream with them. You have to make sure that you do not dance to the tone of their drums again. If you are not strong enough, you can wait for more time when you will be bold enough to tell your story without being judgemental. You don't need to judge anyone, but to advise them about the danger ahead of them if they don't get serious now. You need God's wisdom to talk to them. But guess what? It will be a great thing to do if you have courage to do so. God wants them to experience freedom and his love. They may be thinking that it is cool to be drinking, having fun with sex and drugs. They need a person like you who has been there to let them know that it's not good to do so. It is very dangerous and damaging. You will need a support system – that is, some people to hold you up in prayers and to check on how you are making out. If there is any help I can render, let me know. I will be willing to do so.

As you will soon be preparing for your grade 11 finals, I wish you all the best. You still have about a month to get ready. Continue to draw closer to your mom and dad, youth pastor and above all to Jesus Christ who is able to help you out in all ways. Make sure you talk to him always (I Thess. 5:16-18). God wants you to give thanks to him and to be thankful for who he is in your life. He is able to help you get to where you want to be. I will be expecting your email or phone call. Keep yourself pure in the Lord. He has forgiven your past.

Dear Joe,

Wow Joe! Your parents were so happy that you did so well in your final exams in grade 11. You must be proud of yourself. I don't normally use the word proud, I prefer to say you're blessed; you are being blessed to see the good results of your hard work. I am so glad you have turned your life around like that. I am sure, all things being equal, if your grade 12 result can be as good as grade 11, good scholarships will be waiting for you in any university of your choice. 95% average and above will surely fetch you a good scholarship. More so if you can bring it up a bit more, 96-98%. Is that possible? Nothing is impossible with God (Luke 1:37). Just continue to work smart and leave the result in God's hands. I agree with you that if you attend one of the universities in your city, it will be cheaper for you. Right thinking!

Summer is here. You got a summer job with the city. I hope that will keep you busy and will enable you to save some money for college. I believe you will be a good manager of your money. You don't necessarily need to buy something cheap or on good sale, but something you need. Don't forget, there will be good sales all the time. Many students, before they finish their undergraduate degrees, owe up to $40,000 in student loans. You can easily avoid that by saving money from your summer job, and also by having a good scholarship. You can do it. You are smart enough to achieve your goal, whatever that goal is. When God is on your side, things will be better. "But seek ye first the kingdom of God and his righteousness; and all these things shall be added unto you" (Matt. 6:33) (KJV).

I will also like to advise you to start preparing yourself for university. Although you are planning to stay in your city to attend one of the universities, you still have to decide if you will be staying at home with mom and dad or stay on campus or rent a room. You don't need to be an accountant to know that it will be far cheaper to stay home than to rent a room or live on campus. Pray about it and perhaps talk with your parents. I believe they love you. They want the best for you. Don't focus on the freedom you will get when you leave home. Think on what will be good for your future and make you serious at university. Some first year students waste a lot of their time partying and drinking, because of their so-called "freedom." They may be free from their parents' pressure of dos and don'ts at home, but are they totally free? I don't think so. They think they are free from their parents, but enslave themselves with alcohol, party, sex and so on. Anyway, Joe, think about what you should do, and allow the Holy Spirit to help you to decide. Have a good summer.

Dear Joe,

Yes, Joe, you better believe it, time goes by fast. You are half way through grade 12. I am happy to hear that you had a good summer. You had two jobs, and you were able to save toward your education. Good for you, you are doing better in your studies. You got 98% average in your first semester. Well done, Joe. You are a smart and hard working young man. I am happy for you.

Your parents called me yesterday to inform me that two universities have already given you admissions with good scholarships. Congratulations. I remember you said you want to go to Law school. Have you changed your mind? Have you decided which one of the two universities you are going? Though your parents said you are still waiting for more, the good news is, since you will be working hard, if not harder, for your final marks, scholarships are waiting for you.

You need to have two things in mind; how to maintain your G.P.A. or do better and to choose which university to attend. You cannot go to two universities at a time. The choice is in your hands. At the same time, you have to discuss with your parents, your guidance counsellor and above all, pray about it. Some people like to read Psalm 37 during the time of decision making. All the universities in your city are good. Your mom and dad attended different universities there. I will be praying for God's guidance for you and also for God's favour in anything you do or lay your hands upon. Try to trust him more, he is always there for anyone who patiently wait on him or seek him.

You are planning to attend a youth rally in July. Is it just for your denomination or interdenominational? It will be a good experience for you. You need to prepare yourself fully for university. Spiritually, you really need to be ready. You should know that you are going to a larger community, unlike your high school of about 2,000 students. I will be talking to you during your first months in university. Now you just need to have a good finish in high school.

I will assume that you will be going to the same church after September. Your pastor will be happy to see you doing what you have been doing in the youth group. It is nice to know that you are very active in senior group and in helping out with junior youth. I hope you will continue to be involved in your university years. The more you take part in church activities, the more you grow in the Lord.

Well, I will stop here. I hope to hear from you, especially about your final marks in high school and your final choice of university. Don't worry about anything. Commit your ways unto the Lord and leave the rest in his hands. He will continue to care for you and help you out. May God lead you to make right decisions.

Dear Joe,

Congratulations Joe. I have been thanking God for you continuously. Your final marks were excellent, you got 98.5% average. Good job. The scholarship you got is good for everything you need for your academic year, since you have chosen to stay home. Your choice of university was great. Your mom must be proud that you have chosen hers.

How are you making out? Do you find it different from high school life? More stuff to study. How do you find your professors? You don't need to worry. All you need is to continue with your good work habits. Try to listen to your professors and like them, too. If you like them, it will be easier for you to like their classes. Four years seem to be almost forever, not really, just like high school years. Focus, don't follow multitude to do evil. Jesus calls you the light of the world. You must let your light shine before your course mates, your friends and your professors (Matt. 5:14-16). Continue to be active in your church as usual.

You said you met Abby at the Christian Rally in July. She is a good Christian lady and attending your university. Good for you. She comes from a Christian home - her dad is a deacon in her church. You said she goes to your church and sings in the choir. Good. Your parents must be happy. I believe they like her, right? As of now, both of you have to continue to study smart, try to maintain your stand in the Lord. Be sure to let your friends and course mates know that you are Christians. I hope you will be able to lead some of them to the Lord and let them know what it means to be Christian boy/girlfriend. Be busy with school work, find time to do what is expected of you at church, and at the same time, you will need good quality of time together, especially during the holidays.

Don't be tempted to do what all or many students or girl/boy friends are doing. Your time together is not for drinking or partying and also is not for sexual activities. Remember, you just became friends and also that you are Christians. Other students may do anything they want, you can't. The Spirit of God should teach you what to do, how to behave and how to make yourselves and your bodies pure. You are God's temple (1 Cor. 6:19). Feed your bodies with godly food – the Word of God – and not with immoralities. Remember, if God wants you to be one, you will be able to enjoy everything together. For now, I will suggest you try to enjoy a good friendly relationship and try to correct your friends who are misusing their freedom of being away from home. Christ wants you to represent him in the university. You are both his ambassadors there, among your course mates, friends and student body. I believe Jesus will give you all you need to be good students as well as his ambassadors. God bless you.

Dear Joe,

It has been a while since I've communicated with you in writing. I always enjoy your phone calls. You asked me couple of questions and wanted me to answer you in writing. One, you are wondering if you should go to Law school right away as you will be finishing your undergrad soon. And also Abby's parents are suggesting marriage to both of you.

Your questions have almost the same answer. Are you ready to go to Law school now? Do you have money to carry you through, and also are you ready for a wedding now? Both of you, I believe, have student loans up to $30,000 each. If you get married now, this means your debts will be $60,000, and you will need at least a car, and rent an apartment. I hope you will be able to get good jobs. I will suggest that you find time to talk and pray about these issues. With regard to Law school, if you get admission now, there is nothing wrong for you to do it now; and if Abby is still interested in doing a one year Master degree, it will be good, too. Abby had been promised a bursary by the university, which will be almost enough for the program. She was also promised by a company that she will be able to get a job after her Master degree. That is a good opportunity, which you should not miss. But she has to be ready for it. And since you, too, wanted to do your Law in the same university, it will be a good opportunity to be able to see each other often-as usual. People will say rest is "sweet after labour." If you do all the labour at once, you will be able to rest at last.

Well, what about the wedding? I am not sure why Abby's parents want you to get married now. Is it because they don't want her to miss you? I know there is a danger, sometimes in a long dating. If it is because of that, both of you, you in particular, have to show them that you love her, and you have promised to marry her. Abby's parents think highly of you; explain to them that you will not disappoint her. If you are trying to agree with them because of your belief in abstinent from sex until your wedding, I can't blame you. There is nothing wrong for you to have a small wedding – not too expensive. It is better that way than to go against your conscience and belief. Even though it is the order of the day for boy/girl friends to be sleeping together, even many dating couples are living together for one reason or another. Whatever the reason is, it is not God's principle. And whatever is not God's principle, is wrong. God will not declare something right or wrong because many people are doing it, but according to his own principles. I support your belief and I hope you will think about it seriously. Don't tempt God. Don't go against your conscience and God's teachings. Pray about it. God who has been helping you for the past years – about four now, will continue to give you grace and to uphold you. You will be a good model to your friends and others. Let me know your decisions. God bless you.

Dear Joe,

It is good to know that you both have gone back to studies. Abby will finish her Master degree in one year. Good enough. I believe God will continue to give you strength to say no to the flesh.

You said that you are busier than before. I can imagine. You are co-leaders of the campus Christian Fellowship, and you are having a bible study group at Abby's place for your friends who do not come to your campus fellowship. At the same time, you are still keeping your group leadership in your church, while Abby continues to teach Sunday school. Wow! You are doing great for the Lord. Keep up the good job. But you have to make sure that you have time for your studies as usual. You are spending a lot of time for God, he is a rewarder of those who diligently seek him and are busy for him (Heb.11:6). Don't feel shy to let your friends and Bible study group, also church youth group know your stand with regard to abstinence during dating.

God put you in the university and as leaders of the groups for reasons. Let your light continue to shine and many people will see it and not only give glory to God, but come into the light. There are so many people in darkness in our world today. Many young adults/youth are confused and afraid of their tomorrow. God is using you to be a source of hope for their future. Many people are getting tired of going to church or associating themselves with God. Many have joined different cults or are looking for help where there is none. People like both of you are the hope of the world. Prayerfully, continue to encourage people that if they are on the Lord's side, their tomorrow is safe. I will continue to pray for God's power, wisdom and anointing for you.

Both of you need to continue to find time to seek God's face more than before for his mercy on your relationship and the work he has entrusted into your hands. Find time also to plan and communicate about your future. As you have built yourselves a big empire from a Christian point of view, you should try to uphold each other in prayers and ask your parents on both sides to be praying for you. You have a long way to go, but since God is on your side, victory will always be yours. We need faithful people like you in every walk of life – politics, judiciary, sports, corporations, business, etc. Try your best to be on top. God wants to use you beyond where you are now. I can't wait to see you, Joe, as a Federal Supreme court judge.

May I pray with you? Lord Jesus, thank you for Joe and Abby. Please Lord, continue to bless them in their studies, and their work for you. Make them head in all their endeavours, open doors of opportunities for them, and let divine unprecedented favour be theirs. In Jesus' name. Amen.

Dear Joe,

It is unbelievable that Abby has finished her MBA and worked for about two years now. You, too, just completed your Law degree. Both of you are working for the same Co-operation. You said the Co-operation is good to both of you – salary wise. Good for you. Congratulations for all that God has done for you.

You want me to advise you regarding your wedding. You want to exchange vows next summer. It is good to hear. You are living on the same street about a kilometer apart. Since you are still in the same city, are you planning to go to the same church you were attending when you were in the university? I believe your parents on both sides, Abby's in particular, must be happy to know that you are getting ready to be married. You need to talk and agree on some issues before you say I do; Which Church you will be attending? How big the wedding will be or how much you want to spend? Where is the wedding's venue? Where to honeymoon? Are you ready to buy a house now? How much would you like to spend on the house? What about children? All these questions and others should be addressed.

By the way, I will like to recommend a book to you –"So You're Getting Married: The keys to Building A Strong, Lasting Relationship" by H. Norman Wright. 1985. It is a good book. It will enable you to know how to get ready for the wedding "Day" and also for your marriage. If you cannot find it in the market, let me know, I will loan you a copy. I will advise you to find time to talk more than before; you need to be more open and honest with each other. You need to start dreaming together about the kind of marriage you would like to have. Each one of you have to ask yourself: what am I bringing into this relationship? Am I ready to spend the rest of my life with this man/woman? Am I ready to commit myself into an unbreakable relationship? what kind of changes and adjustments do I need to make? I don't mean to scare you about marriage. It is a good relationship God himself instituted. Since he said, it is not good for a man to be alone, I will make him a good helper (Gen 2:18), he knows that both of you need each other, and I believe his hands are in your relationship. Pray to him to make it work or ask him what you need – both of you as well as each one of you – to do to make your intended marriage work. Do not be scared. God will start it for you and he will be there for you. Talk to him about your dreams and all aspects of your prospective home. Say hi to Abby. I promise you my prayers. God bless you.

Dear Joe and Abby,

What a wonderful wedding! Joe, your parents called me and told me how happy they were about everything concerning the occasion. I would like to congratulate both of you. You made it. I pray for God's blessing on your new home that has been built on the Rock - Jesus Christ.

A proverb says, "The wisdom/energy/design one used to build a house is different from the way to live in the house." The Good news is our God is the same. He is the one who helped you to build your marriage. He knows how to sustain it. He is the author of marriage. Don't wait until things are out of control before you talk to him. Ask for wisdom to live with each other and to enable you to commit your whole selves into your marriage. Make every day your honeymoon. Continue to water what you have planted during your courtship or date. Joe, make sure that you are the same Joe that Abby married and Abby needs to be the same as well. The change you need to make should be for the betterment of your marriage not the other way around. Be of one mind. You are no more two, you are one. Don't allow anything, any circumstances to divide you. Go on your knees together before God. A prayerful couple is a powerful couple, and a prayer-less couple is a powerless couple; more prayer, more power, less prayer, less power. You don't need to allow a situation to drag you to God in prayer, but pray to God to prevent a bad situation. In the Lord's prayer- Jesus taught us to say lead us not into temptation, but deliver us from evil (Matt. 6:13). Jesus addresses both the future (lead us not into temptation) and present (deliver us from evil). You have to prepare yourselves for a rainy day. Pray and work ahead of turbulent times in marriage. Find time to study the word of God and pray together.

Since you will be attending the same church you attended before your wedding, I will suggest that you join a new couples group. If none is available in your church, talk to your pastor and ask if one could be started. If you have to start a group, I will be able to give you books on marriage. I'm glad that you enjoyed and found Dr. H. Norman Wright's book very helpful. I have some of his other books. The one on communication is super. I have other books by other authors. Let me know, if you will be in charge or otherwise. I believe that you are aware that you will need some adjustments and changes. Make changes for each other's sake and for your marriage. For any aspects of change or adjustment you may find or might have found difficult, do not hesitate to talk to God for yourself or for your wife/husband. It was a big adjustment for Jesus to leave his glorious house to come to the world. When you talk to him about a change or adjustment he should understand, he has been there. I pray for more of God in your new home. Surely, he will give you all you need to be a couple after his own heart. Focus on good families in the bible and try to study about them. God bless you more.

Dear Joe and Abby,

It seems to me that you are enjoying your marital life. God is always right. He says: "It is not good for a man to be alone. I will make a helper suitable for him"(Gen. 2:18) (NIV). You will agree that "two are better than one" (Eccles. 4:9)). I wish you a long and productive marital life together.

In our discussion on the phone the other time, I could sense that you are not doing badly with regard to your sexual life. I don't need to remind you that your life is now different from your single life. You have disciplined yourselves with regard to immoralities. Now, you are free to have sexual intercourse any time you want. You should not deprive each other from having it. Paul the apostle in God's wisdom says: "The husband should fulfill his marital duty to his wife, and likewise the wife to her husband. The wife's body does not belong to her alone but also to her husband. In the same way, the husband's body does not belong to him alone but also to his wife. Do not deprive each other except by mutual consent and for a time, so that you may devote yourselves to prayer. Then come together again so that Satan will not tempt you because of your lack of self-control. I say this as a concession, not as a command" (1Cor. 7: 3-6) (NIV).

I will encourage you to meditate on Apostle Paul's advice. Your individual body belonged to you before you said "I do." After the exchange of your vows, it does not remain the same. Your bodies belong to each other and to God. In all you do, let your bodies give glory to God. Do not be like many couples who fight a lot, or abuse their partners or punish their husband/wife with regard to sexual intercourse. Do it and let the glory of God be seen in your relationship. By this, people around you would know that you love each other. Sex is a key element in promoting love between a husband and wife.

I hope you have not been having any issue about sexual relations. If not, that is super, if yes, quickly resolve it and do what is right. God wants you to be in good terms all the time and in every situation. Talk about it, agree on how often you want to enjoy it, and both of you should be ready for it. Don't do it only because of your partner but also because of yourself. Exercise your freedom and do it in a way to bring happiness, joy and satisfaction into your marriage. Many marriages today dissolve due to lack of affectionate passion with regard to sexual relationship. God loves you, he cares for you and he wants the best for your marriage. You need to say thank you to him through your love for each other. I will be looking forward to hearing from you. Keep well. God bless you always.

Dear Abby and Joe,

I got a letter form Abby about a week ago. I understand that you have stopped helping out at church as Sunday school teachers and youth leaders. You have been waiting for a couple of years to be blessed with the fruit of the womb. Because of this, you started to be angry with God. And Joe has started drinking again.

You told me that doctors didn't find anything wrong with both of you and that they don't know why you haven't been able to conceive. I can sense some anger and frustration in you. Are you disappointed with God? You have been serving God faithfully and you expect him to be good to you in all aspects of life. I am wondering, if you told your pastor or if he came to you to find out why you stopped going to church or unable to do what you have been doing in the church. I would like to suggest to you that anger is not the solution to your problems. I'm wondering if the situation is not affecting you relationships, and also affecting you at work.

The devil is always happy when a child of God is experiencing difficulties and he/she starts to be angry with him/herself, at life and above all angry with God. We Christians are not supposed to serve God because of what we want from him, but because of his attributes. He is holy, he's powerful, he's able to do all things etc. He loves you and wants you to carry all your problems, and anxiety to him because he cares for you (Ps. 55:22 and 1Peter 5:7).

God wants us to come to him and express our feelings to him. He is able to solve all your problems. I know you have been looking forward to having children and you think it is not fair that you haven't had any for the past 3 years. It will be a good idea to go back to God and tell him that you are sorry. If your pastor and friends have not joined you in prayer or prayed for you, I will advise that you call on them to pray, since this situation seems to be greater than what medical solutions can handle. God is able to do all things. Don't try to solve the problems in your own way. Remember, Abraham and Sarah tried to solve their problem of barrenness, but they ended up in adding to their problems. Abraham found himself between two wives and rivalry ensued. Since God said be fruitful and multiply, he knows how to let that happen in your life. I will join you in prayer. Let us trust that he will help you out soon.

Joe, what does getting back to alcohol produce? I can guess that you want it to make you forget the issue. Yes, temporary solution is good, but the best is to find a means to overcome the unpleasant situation. It is not fun to be back to the old nature; for a dog to go back to his vomit is not the appropriate way out. Proverb

26:11 declares: "As a dog returns to its vomit, so fool repeats his folly"- this is not to say that you're a fool. Drinking will not take away the problem, and it can worsen the scenario. Continuously talk to God who has a lasting solution to your problem. God is the same today, yesterday and forever; he will never change (Heb. 13:8). As he delivered you from the grip of alcohol in the past, he will release you from it again and grant you the desires of your heart. He is still the Almighty God. I want you to return to him and tell him about your predicament, he is the answer to all problems. Paul the Apostle said: "Do not be anxious about anything, but in everything, by prayer and petition, with thanksgiving, present your request to God" (Phil. 4:6) (NIV). May God listen to your prayers.

Dear Joe and Abby,

I'm so pleased that Abby is 2 months pregnant. You have been to the Gynecologist and he confirmed it. I am so happy for you. The atmosphere in your home is getting better. The Lord is good to you. 7 months ago, when I wrote you a letter, I was the only one who believed that the Lord is able. But I did not envisage that it would be quick like this. Congratulations. I am hoping that Abby will be taken it easy.

Since you got what you were angry about and fighting for, I would like to see your life come back to normal completely. Joe, I'm glad that your joy is back and that your cravings for alcohol have been reduced. Your baby needs to see you and his/her mom being happy together. In order to have a happy and joyful baby, as parents, you must possess what your child needs. You don't need to wait till the arrival of the baby before you fall in love again. He/she will need both of you to stick together and work toward welcoming him/her. I would like to encourage you to go back to your pastor for prayer. I am delighted to hear that you have started going back to church and to your volunteer jobs there. Good for you. God wants your love and care for each other to be better than before. For almost a year, you had a rough time. The rough time is supposed to be over as happy and joyous times are back.

God has turned your anger and frustration into joy and laughter. Since he has granted your petitions, you have to show your appreciation by being thankful always. You are blessed to have good parents on both sides supporting you. Your church and friends also took the situation upon themselves. I joined you and your parents, Church and friends to thank God on your behalf. Let there be a major turn-around in your attitude toward each other and genuine love for God.

You should be able to know the sex of the baby through the ultrasound, perhaps after some weeks or months. I'll be looking forward to knowing and I can't wait to congratulate you on the arrival of the baby. Just try to let go of the offences toward each other. The tension was too much between you because your expectations, particularly fertility, did not materialize on time. But now that the tension is gone, your joy should be back. The gift of children in any marriage is a plus. The most important element for any marriage to survive is love. Love is the language that the blind can see and the deaf can hear. This is what you need to plan to welcome your child with. He/she needs love from both of you. You can only give what you have. Try to have love and to show it to each other. God loves you and he wants you to love each other and to prepare to show love to your baby who is to come. God bless you. Stay in touch.

Dear Joe and Abby,

Wow!! You have a set of twins. Congratulations to you and your parents on both sides. You must be so busy. Jenna and Bob's arrival into your home must make you a blessed couple. God made a double blessing for you. How are you making out at nights? Do they sleep through? How about feeding? Do you breast feed and supplement with infant formula? You are blessed that your parents on both sides live within 3 hour drive from you. I hope you'll keep them busy, particularly Abby's mom.

Now that you have gotten what you have been waiting for, you have to demonstrate some kind of parental roles in the lives of the twins. The book of Proverbs says: "Train a child in the way he should go and when he is old he will not turn from it" (Proverb 22:6) (NIV). God has been so generous to you by giving you a double portion of blessings. God trusts that you will be able to show these children real love. As God is Love, he wants you to love each other and to pass it on to your children. You need genuine love and at the same time, the twins need undivided attention. Your care for them should be equal. Let them grow up to see you fall in love every time. The surpassing love God has for the world made his son, Jesus Christ, come and die for the sin of humanity. You have to love each other unconditionally as God in Jesus Christ loves you. This love, agape, is what you need. Try as much as possible to forget about the past. Those 18 months or so of fights, arguments, anger, and other negative emotions have already passed by. Let unconditional love over-shadow the rough time. True love covers a multitude of sins, mistakes, offences and such things. I'm wondering if you are familiar with first Corinthians 13. I will encourage you to read it, digest it and apply it to your marital life. Let me quote verse 2, where Paul says "if I have the gift of prophecy and fathom all mysteries and all knowledge and I have a faith that can move mountains, but have not love, I'm nothing." (ICor.13:2) (NIV).

Do not wait until the twins grow up before you start teaching them what love is and how to feel and show love. You're the first teachers of your children, you'll be teaching them by words, deeds, actions, and etc. Remember, you can only give what you have or teach what you know. Since both of you came from good, loving Christian homes, you need to pass it on to your children. I believe you can do it. Let the beauty of the Lord be seen in you. If you have any questions, give me a ring.

Let me pray with you. Our Lord God, thank you for your faithfulness, thank you for the gifts of the twins and also for taking good care of them. We pray that you will bless Abby and Joe with all they need to be good parents and meet all their other needs.

Dear Joe and Abby,

I'm glad to know that you have been having fun with the twins. You said that your lives have been richly blessed. I'm glad to hear that. God gave you the twins as free gifts and you really appreciate him for his generosity to you. It's good to know that you dedicated them to God in your church last week. I believe God will continue to keep watch over them. You said on the phone that you are doing much better and that your love for each other is growing, good for you. As requested, I'm writing to briefly discuss forgiveness.

According to 1Cor. 13:5; love is always ready to forgive, it does not keep record of wrongs and it is also not easily angered. I believe that you have spoken about the past, and each one of you has asked for forgiveness. If you haven't, it will be good to talk about it briefly. It shouldn't be characterized by self-defense, accusation or fault finding, but to ask for forgiveness. The tension between you combined with work demands, infertility issue, pressure from friends and parents-are behind you now. You need to turn a new page and try to be like children. Children have a short memory of yesterday's offenses. They find it easy to forgive and forget. Bitterness and anger are not supposed to have room in your family.

As Abby is still breast feeding, I would suggest that anger and frustration should not have a place in her life. Joy, happiness, contentment, peace, hope, love and all good things are the states in which she is supposed to be, and perhaps all the time. When you both carry the twins or want to play with them, they need to see that kind of joy and sense of forgiveness in both of you. Don't be deceived, the children know what is going on, they learn so quickly. Let them see you as loving, caring parents and above all, let them see you as one.

I believe you've taught forgiveness before, either in the Sunday school or in the youth group. It is time for you to teach yourselves individually, how God has forgiven you and washed you from your sins through the blood of Jesus Christ. God has forgiven you. Forgive each other whole-heartedly so that your prayers will not be hindered. Your marital life, shortly after wedding was good. You seemed to be happy and communicated with each other a lot and even effectively. You need to go back to that time of happy married life. If there is any time for you to be happy together, it is now. May the Lord bless you, as you are engaged in the process of forgiveness and work on letting go of the past, peace of Christ be with you.

Dear Joe and Abby,

I don't need to be told that things are going on well with you. Your love for each other is back and you have humbled yourselves to say I am sorry to each other. The arrival of your new son tells me that you are doing great. And I am happy that things are fantastic with you. Joe was promoted recently and your house had been fully paid off. Double congratulations!

Now that everything is back to normal, I would like to advise you to keep the flag flying. It was nice to hear about your forthcoming 10th wedding anniversary plans. You're planning to go to Bermuda. Good for you. Bermuda is a lovely place, I've been there. Spending a week there, will enable you to really enjoy the country. It is somehow expensive there, but you deserve a big timeout and more so that it is a romantic getaway. I hope you will not miss your children too much. It's great that Joe's parents would be honored to help you out. Well, you still have 9 months before you go, Jim will be almost one year old.

There must be some couples you know that are still in the "dark" with regard to their marital lives. Pray to God for direction on how you can help them out in anyway. You have been there; you know how miserable it is for a couple without children or harmony. It is frustrating. God did not create marriage for separation or destruction. He wants couples to be in love, live happily and to be one. Don't be too shy to share your testimony with your friends and coworkers; about where you were, what brought you there and how God brought an end to your fight. Many marriages end today, because there are inadequate role model couples to mentor new ones. Maybe God allowed the frustrations in your marriage to enable you to help others. Pray about it, if I can help in any way, let me know. Divorce rate in our society today is not good, and some things must be done about it. God will not come down from heaven to help troubled married couples. People like you and me have to do whatever we can to help. May God lead you rightly as you ponder and pray about it.

Abby and Joe, I would like to thank you for the opportunity I have had to come into your marital-life. I trust the Holy Spirit will guide you in your decision and enable you to do God's Will. Have a wonderful marital life. May you and your children be a blessing to others.

Let me pray with you. Lord, I pray that you will please bless Joe, Abby and the children. Let the children continue to grow in your knowledge, and meet the needs of this family. Let them continue to be a good role model to many families, in Jesus name. Amen.

Chapter 16
Noah and Lori – A Couple with Gambling/Casino Addiction

Dear Noah & Lori,

Greetings. We had a good and long talk, when I met you last week. I promised to put my thoughts in writing. As both of you have said you met at a casino. You used to play together and as time went by you became good friends, and eventually started dating. You got married nine years ago. You have two kids; a 6 year old and a 4 year old. You have been blessed with good jobs with - six figure salaries. Good for you.

I am concerned for both of you, because you spend 50% of you combined income on gambling. You buy lottery tickets regularly and you still visit casino in your city, sometimes together and most of the time Lori goes by herself. Noah you said you have been trying to stop gambling but since Lori is still heavily involved, it is not easy on you. I can understand Lori is not happy with you for not gambling with her or going to the casino to play. You have been buying lottery tickets for years and you have never won more than $5000. You said you are not that lucky! You don't always get the outcome you want while at the casino either. Gambling is a game of chance. You have been taken chances for years without a significant result. Each day or week you always think that your chance is on the way. When is it going to be your time?

Noah, it seems to me that you're aware that something is wrong. You are not driving a befitting car and you are hardly able to pay your bills, you are also behind on your mortgage payments. According to you, workers under you at work are more financially stable than you are. Noah's parents have been worrying about your life style. They always pray to God to help you out. You said you always laugh at them. As I suggested to you last time, you sat down and calculated how much you spend on casino, gambling and lottery every week, and multiplied that by four weeks and then by twelve months. Your calculations indicate that you're spending more than $70,000 every year on something that is not rewarding. Is it not time for you to think and plan for your future? I hope and pray that both of you will have your jobs until your retirement, assuming that you do, what about your children? They are very young but getting older every year. What plan do you have for them or for your future?

Noah you mentioned that you have tried to quit for about two weeks or so and that you have not been spending a lot lately. You are confused and tired of life. You cannot control or stop your habit. Who will deliver you? That's what you are wondering about. To be honest with you, it is not that easy to break a habit or stop an addiction more so that Lori is still fully involved. Noah, you have to stand-alone and stand tall. Both of you need God through Jesus Christ to help you out. Paul the apostle used to struggle with sin many years ago and noted: "We know that the law is spiritual; but I am unspiritual, sold as a slave to sin. I do not understand what I do. For what I want to do I do not do, but what I hate I do. And if I do what I do not want to do, I agree that the law is good. As it is, it is no longer I myself who do it, but it is sin living in me. I know that nothing good lives in me, that is, in my sinful nature. For I have the desire to do what is good, but I cannot carry it out. For I do not do the good I want to do; no, the evil I do not want to do—this I keep on doing. Now if I do what I do not want to do, it is no longer I who do it, but it is sin living in me that does it. So I find this law at work: When I want to do good, evil is right there with me. For in my inner being, I delight in God's law; but I see another law at work in the members of my body, waging war against the law of my mind and making me a prisoner of the law of sin at war within my members. What a wretched man I am! Who will rescue me from this body of death? Thanks be to God-through Jesus Christ our Lord! So then, I myself in my mind am a slave to God's law, but in my sinful nature a slave to the law of sin." (Romans 7:14-25)(NIV).

Jesus Christ set Paul free from the bondage of Satan. You, too, need to be like Paul. God is able to set both of you free at the same time or one by one. Pray to God to come back into your life. You stopped going to church, you need to start all over again. God is waiting for you. I will get in touch again.

Dear Noah and Lori,

It's amazing that Noah's mom read the book of Romans to you specifically chapter 7:14-25 and chapter 8. In fact that was God incident and not a coincident. It must be a divine passage for you. I am glad to know that the passage spoke to you a lot. Was it the same with Lori? You said you have seen a big difference in your finances.

Since you have prayed a breakthrough prayer with your parents and you believed you have been set free from satanic bondage of gambling, I will suggest that you continue to pray for Lori. Do not judge her or condemn her, just share with her what it means to be set free. Let her also know how much you both would save as a family since you have totally stopped gambling, buying lottery tickets, and playing at casino. As you said you are eating well and on time- no more junk food. You can see the difference in your body. You did not realize that you are sort of an alcoholic. You used to drink a lot while gambling at casino. You have been set free form alcoholism, too. Praise God for that. "So if the Son sets you free, you will be free indeed" (John 8:36) (NIV). Enjoy your freedom in the Lord.

Noah, I am wondering what you have been doing with your extra time. I believe you told me before that your day used to start at 7am and end around 9 or 10pm. You usually left work for the casino. I am hoping you will let your children see a big change in you. Time is the best and most precious investment you can make on your children. Your children are used to daycare and a baby sitter. It would be better, if you can be home after work, pick up the children from daycare so that your 4 year old daughter will no longer be there from morning till 5 or 6pm when the baby sitter used to pick them up from daycare. Let them have a good supper with you every day. Spend some time with them before they go to bed. Maybe you can involve them in sports in the evenings. The time you will spend with them is an investment. The money you will spend on their sport events is more rewarding than your previous wasteful spending – on casino, gambling etc. Spend time and money wisely on your children, you will never regret it.

At least, one of you is home now with the children to say goodnight to them, reading them stories with prayers before they go to bed. I hope your marital relationship and your children will be a priority. Continue to do your best to be one. Care for each other. Don't forget you are one body. Your children would be happy to see you together and doing things with them. It would be good if you can be spending the weekend together as a family. Going to the park, church, even cooking and eating together will increase sense of family-hood in the children. I know they had been used to not seeing you around in the evenings and most of the weekends – even though things are changing since Noah has been coming home after work – but they will be happy to see a big change. I am sure, they will feel a sense of love, affection, and above all the relationship with them will be stronger.

I am hoping to hear from you soon. I will be away for a couple of weeks. But if you have any questions you can email me. I will be thinking of you. God bless.

Dear Noah

Greetings. I got your letter when I came home from my trip. Lori has been coming home later than before and most of the nights she is heavily drunk! I would not be surprised if she has been spending more money than before. Noah, you are wondering what you should do. She is still working hard and receiving promotion at work. You said that your mind is not clear about her boss. He is her gambler buddy and they had been spending a lot of time together at the casino.

Have you been having a good time to talk? If yes, let her know how you are feeling, especially with regards to being with her boss after work. There is nothing wrong in letting her know that she has been disturbing the whole family, each night she comes home. She needs to be told that she is still your wife and a mom to her/your children. Prayerfully, encourage her to discipline herself and to try to taste freedom from her gambling/habit. If she doesn't have time for verbal communication – since she has been coming home late every night, you may write her a comprehensive letter or an email. Let her know what I have said and how you are feeling. This is not an avenue of judgment on her or I am better or holier than you. Remember, you had been there before. Be sincere, but do it in love. By the way, do you still love her? Love covers a multitude of sins. If your love for her is still there and strong, the best you can do is to pray for her every day. How can you express your love toward her, since she is not home almost all the time and when she comes home, she is not herself as she is half drunk. Pray to God to teach you what to do and how you need to represent him in Lori's life, since she still comes home, sees herself as your wife and the mom of your children. If Jesus is her earthly husband, I wonder what he would do. It is not too much to ask him what he would do. Ask him to give you courage and patient to do the same.

God told the prophet Hosea to love his unlovable wife, Gomer. The more Gomer enjoyed her adulteress life, the more Hosea loved her. God told Hosea, "Go show your love to your wife again, though she is loved by another and is an adulteress. Love her as the Lord loves the Israelites, though they turn to other gods and love the sacred raisin – cakes." (Hosea 3:1) (NIV). God's love for us is unconditional. He wants you to do the same for Lori. Your mom and dad prayed for you for years. Their prayers have been answered. Ask them to join you in praying for her. Since God was able to help you to get over the addiction, he is able to do the same for Lori. Write her a note or an email and express your love for her. Beware, don't judge her, but let her know that you are praying for her and that you and the kids are missing her nightly at home. Plan a getaway weekend, and let her know in advance. The more you love her and try to tolerate her and accept her unconditionally, the more she may likely feel good about herself and feel accepted. "Welcome, how was your day?" "How are your co-workers treating you as their new boss?" etc. These kinds of greeting and questions will enable her to know that you care for her. Express your feelings and love in written form clearly and boldly and put it on her side of the bed. Pray and wait to welcome her home in the real sense. You know what I mean? Expect her to come and resume her duties as a wife and mom. I will write her a letter. Pray for me. My prayers are with you. Be blessed in the Lord. How are the children? Give my love to them.

Dear Lori,

I was told you are being promoted at work! Congratulations. I am happy for you and your family. You are now one of the decision makers for the company.

How are you feeling since Noah stopped gambling with you? It has been a long time since you have been gambling partners. Do you feel lonely sometimes? Are you mad at him sometimes? I believe you met each other at a casino and all of a sudden, he left you. He does not want you to talk about it and show no interest in how much you won or lost and doesn't want to know about the new gambling friends.

I am not really sure if you know what is going on in your family. Noah is not happy that his wife is not at home every night and most of the weekends. She is not there either for him or the children. He told me that you have been spending a lot of time during and after gambling with your boss. Your boss drives you home some of the nights because you drink heavily. Is that true? It seems to me that you have replaced Noah with your boss. Since Noah is no longer your gambling buddy, and drinking partner, your boss stepped in. Is that a good replacement? I understand also that your boss' wife left him a couple of months ago. Did she leave when she suspected that you're going out with her husband? When you made your vows at your wedding, the pastor read to you that what God has joined together let no man separate. Gambling/casino, drinking and your boss are trying to separate you from your husband and the commitments you have made to him and your marriage. What about your children? They are practically being raised by a single parent.

Thank God you have a good job with a fantastic salary. Your spending has been increased due to heavy drinking and more gambling and lottery play. You have been waiting for the time when you will win a lot of money. It is good to be a millionaire, but after that what? What will it profit a person when he/she wins a big lottery or big money through gambling,to use the biblical phrase, and loses his/her soul(Mark 8:36). In your own case, what will be your gain after winning big money which you have never won for the past ten years I believe – and lose your family? Your parents as well as your siblings do not care about you any longer. Your children have stopped asking for their mom.

You have to divorce one thing - either your family including your extended family or your addiction. I will like you to think about it. Your parents were there for you, they gave you all they could and paid for your education - up to your PhD degree without a student loan. They financed your wedding and gave you a down payment on your mortgage. What else can good parents do? You knew about the

Lord since you were 4 years old. I am not saying all this to make you feel guilty or bad about yourself, but to think about the outcome of what you are doing. If you are not there for your kids, what stories do you want them to tell about you to their own children? I believe it is not too late. It will be great for you, if you can find time to talk with Noah and ask him how he overcame his own addiction and what's keeping him going. It is not too late for you to turn things around. It just needs courage to say enough is enough! Your future is bright with your family, if you can invite the light of the world, Jesus Christ, into your life again. God loves you and so do I. God bless.

Dear Noah & Lori,

How are things with you these days? It's nice to know that Lori has been doing some soul searching. In fact, our conversation on the phone last week gave me some hope that things are getting better slowly but surely.

You need to talk more and the only way to have time to talk is for Lori to make her-self more available. You have been trying and I thank God for you. Try to discipline yourself more. I know from our conversation that you have reduced your alcohol intake and come home earlier than before. You said that it isn't easy to just stop like that! If you really want to be there for your children and be part of their development, you have to take a radical step in your thinking. You should not wait until your first child is a teenager and by this time next year she will be a pre-teen. This is your time to restore what you have stolen from them. You should be there for them and be a mom that they have never had. You can think of going for treatment at a detox center or anywhere but I am not sure if that will not affect you at work. Your job is so important but your family- husband, your children in particular, are also very essential in your life. If you think that going to a detox center will somehow belittle you at work, another action you can take is a dramatic spiritual turn around. How can that be? You may ask.

Spiritual turnaround step worked for Noah. Talk to him and pray together, discipline yourself and take an unprecedented step, that is, replace addiction with your children/family. You can't change yourself. Nobody will do it for you except God. I can sense that you may likely be powerless over the addiction, but God is powerful. He has power over you and your addiction. He is wiser than the wisest. Call on him. He is more than willing to help you and set you free. Jesus Christ was born to set those who are in the bondage of sin free. He has been doing so for about 2000 years. He has done so for so many people including myself, yours will not be exceptional. Talk to him, tell him everything about you, and all you have wasted – money and time in particular. He is able to forgive you and forget and make a new Lori out of the old. Humble yourself to ask Noah to join you in prayer.

Noah, you need to accept Lori as she is undergoing the process of a change in her life. You need to take it easy with her and understand where she is coming from as you have also been there. Two are always better than one (Eccles. 4:9). You should be thankful to God for what is happening now in Lori's life. This is what you have been praying and waiting for. It is almost there. Be patient and accommodating. If Lori can settle with God first, that is, seek and receive forgiveness from God, It will be easier for her to ask for forgiveness from you, and the children. I will be talking about forgiveness and how to be one again. Pray, and read the bible together. Let the word of God be your guide to righteous living and pray to live a holy life. The family that prays together will stay together. United we stand, divided we fall. Let God stand and let the devil fall under your feet. Victory is yours in Jesus. Keep in touch. God bless you richly.

Dear Noah & Lori,

I am impressed to hear about all the good things that have been happening in your home. The children are happier and able to see their mom most of the nights before they sleep. You have been praying together and communicating often. I was delighted to hear that Lori went on a self-retreat. You were also able to rededicate your lives to God. Even though it has not been easy on you as you mentioned during our telephone conversation, but God's grace for each day has been sufficient for you.

Both of you are now in the same boat. You have been going to bed together almost every night. Lori, you have been worried about your past. You said you are ashamed of yourself and that you did not know how dirty you were until you went to your wake up retreat weekend. Yes, you must have been dirty, but that is the Lori of the past. You have now been cleaned by the blood of Jesus Christ. God has forgiven you and Noah had a long talk and time of sharing. You asked for forgiveness from him and he did the same to you. Since God has forgiven both of you and you have forgiven each other, the rest is easy. You do not need to dwell in the past. That is by gone. Try to make good use of your present and plan for your future. By the way, Lori, did you speak with your children and apologize to them? Your parents also need to forgive you for what they have gone through emotionally among their friends and extended family members, even in the church. Lori you need to take a step further. You ought to forgive yourself. It is easy to accept God and others' forgiveness, but it is not that easy to forgive one-self. Close that long chapter in your life and open a new one. Trust God to make your new dream come true with regard to having a Godly family.

Both of you tried to blame yourselves for your wastefulness regarding the money and time you have spent on gambling and alcohol consumption. Again, that was in the past. I thank God that you did not lose your jobs. You were hopeful. Life has a different meaning, now. You almost lost your marriage. It was dying, in fact, it was dead, but the application of your marital God's lifetime warranty saved it. When was the last time you enjoyed yourself sexually? Or had a good relationship as husband and wife? When was your last getaway? It's amazing that you were lost or almost lost, but now you are found. Your marriage has been resurrected. The disciples of Jesus Christ didn't fully appreciate their Lord (Jesus) until after his resurrection. I hope the same principle will happen to your marriage. Try to make it the way God wanted or planned it to be. Talk more to him and let him talk to you through his Holy Book. You could be a light in the darkness. You have tested both and you know the difference. So let your light so shine before your friends, co-workers, and couples in your community and church.

Now that you will be having all your income, you need to plan how to manage your finances. God is going to bless you, just continue to be on his side. He will neither leave you nor forsake you. He is going to be all in all to you. Do not forget to bless your children with your time. Time is the best investment parents can make on their children. Invest it wisely and meaningfully. Above all, carry them before the throne of God daily. I pray for more of him in your lives. I will be expecting feedback from you. God bless.

Dear Lori & Noah,

You are more than welcome. I, too, appreciate you so much. I am thanking God daily for you for the major turnaround in your lives and your marital life. What a big change. I was able to hear you laughing aloud during our phone conversation. I can sense the joy of the Lord in you. You made me strongly believe more that money can only buy happiness -in your own case, even money did not buy happiness, but instead, sadness! When Christ was born more than 2000 years ago, the angel announced joy to the world (Luke 2:10). I trust you and Christ in you that the joy you are having now will be permanent in your home, in Jesus name.

For the first time ever, you went on a 2 week holiday with the kids. I can only imagine what is going on in their minds. They must be happy that their dreams are coming true. Each fall, at the beginning of school year, your kid's friend used to tell them where they went for their vacation. Your kids would now have some stories to tell their friends, too. They must be glad. The kids love their Sunday school and both of you love sitting together on the pew every Sunday. I am so thankful for you. Noah, you said you have been asked to serve on the board at your church, while Lori is thinking of joining the choir. She has a beautiful voice and Noah you will be able to use your knowledge to bless the church. It is good that you are trying to bless God's work through the gifts that he has given you. Good job, friends.

I am wondering if you would like to consider starting a kind of educational program in your church. It may be something on how we can be a good steward of what God has blessed us with. There is possibility of having many "old Noah and Lori" on the pews. Many marriages are suffering in silence. Pastor or pastors cannot do it all by themselves. Many kids are without parents at home nightly. None of the parents are there to say goodnight – to give the kids hugs and kisses. Some parents are not home because they have to work, but there are many who are not there for their kids because of one addiction or the other. They are making their addiction a priority over their kids. Parents should be good stewards of their children. What about money? Financial mismanagement among couples is unbelievable. Waste of life, waste of time and wasteful spending should be stopped. How? Someone like you who have seen the light ought to do something about it. Pray about it and if I can be of any help to you, let me know. We were saved to serve.

Talking about your past to others and teaching others how to live will not only save many marriages or help many kids; it will also help you grow more in love and in the Lord. The Holy Spirit will teach you what to teach others. He will also help your prayer life. As you will be praying about the program and the participants you will be praying for yourselves, too. More prayer more power, less prayer less power. When we pray, we are trying to tear down the stronghold of the devil. He is under your feet. That is where he belongs. Help others to allow Jesus to put the devil under their feet, too.

Indeed you are a great couple and I am so blessed to know you and to work with you. Let me close my last letter with you with the saying of Jesus Christ, which is called the beatitudes. He says: "You are the light of the world. A city set on a hill cannot be hidden"... let people see your good work, so they may praise your father in heaven (Matt 5:14-16) (NIV). Is it okay to share your stories with others, perhaps without disclosing your name? I'm just a telephone call away, so keep in touch. God cares for you because he loves you, and so do I.

Chapter 17
Jim and May – Pornography Issue

Dear May & Jim,

Thank you for your letter. It must be tough for both of you! If I can recollect, when I met you, Jim, you said you have been having problems with pornography for so many years. The addiction started when you were 9 years old. Your dad used to subscribe to a magazine with some minor pornography and you used to enjoy looking at them. Later on, in your life, you found yourself chatting on the internet and visiting pornographic sites. You said you have a lot of children, young people and adults naked or half naked pictures.

When I asked you how May had been coping with you for the past five years of your marriage and why she did not make her concerns known to you before now. May said she never knew that you were interested in pornography. During your dating, Jim, you tried to hide all the pictures both on your laptop and desktop computer. You have tried to hide yourself for so many years. You have forgotten that the eyes of the Lord are everywhere keeping watch on both the evil and good people (Prov. 15:3). As I said to you during our meeting, you cannot run away from the truth forever. Inside you, you knew that what you were doing was not good, but you did not know how to get out of the cage until you were cut at the airport during a random checking. You blame yourself for carrying your laptop with you with heavy loads of pornography. You admitted that was not the first time of flying with the same laptop. Why now? To me, it seems like God wanted something to be done about it.

Jim has been arrested and charged. The court hearing is on the way. May, you expressed your frustration, anger and embarrassment to me. You said you were so ashamed of yourself as well as your family. I am wondering how the situation is affecting your marital life. May, according to your words: "It has been hell around here." Are you upset about the court-hearing date? I can sense that it is not easy on both of you. You asked Jim in my presence if he has your "naked" photos as well as your daughter's. Even though Jim said no, it seems like you don't trust his response. Both of you need to focus on the court hearing date and what will come out of it. Continue to talk to your lawyer, and we'll wait and see. The first step Jim needs to take is to admit that he is wrong. He made a mistake and he has to deal with it. He has destroyed the trust you built in him. Your three-year-old girl does not deserve this. How are your parents on both sides coping, especially Jim's parents?

By the way you have spoken to me and in your letter I can feel that the tension in your home is not only affecting your marriage, it is also affecting your spiritual life. Where is God in this situation? May, you said, you are a woman of faith and your prayer life suggests that to me. But for the past few weeks, things have not been the same. Jim and May, there is nothing too beautiful or too ugly we cannot talk to God about. Do not be too shameful to talk to him. He is our present help in the time of trouble. He is more than ready to help you out. Let me know how things are going.

Dear Jim & May,

How are things with you? Thanks for your phone calls and letter. I can't blame Jim's parents for being so angry, especially his mom. May, both of your parents were so angry about the situation as well as with Jim. They have not been talking to him on the phone any time they call. They are thinking they have a disappointing son-in-law! I hope that in time Jim would prove himself a trustworthy person. We don't need to spend much of our energy on that. Let us face the court case, one situation at a time.

Jim went for a court hearing last week. Sentencing will take place by the end of next month. Jim's lawyer advised Jim to plead guilty. Let's wait and see what the court outcome will be. Jim has been banned from being with children by himself. Jim you have a long way to go. The best step for you to take is to realize that you have over stepped your boundary of trust. You need to build the bridge of trust with May and your daughter. Your parents -in-law are disappointed with you. What about your own parents? The first step to take is to start all over and trust yourself that you will come out of this big mess. You need to forgive yourself and try to learn how to be totally free from any unlawful thing. You have lost some of your freedom and wondering how much jail time you will get. You felt bad that your wife has to be there by herself looking after your girl. I don't want to mention her name because I don't know where this letter will be or who may have the chance to read it. You also felt bad that you may not likely be around when your son is born. You are expecting your son to be born in three months. You do not want your children to have a record that their dad has been to jail and that their mom would not be proud that her husband is in jail, especially in the hospital when the baby is born. You are also concerned that your parents and parents- in-law are deeply disappointed with you. To be frank, Jim, many people don't think about the outcome of what they are doing – wrong deeds in particular. The bible is very clear about that. The book of Deuteronomy 32 verse 29 says: "O that they were wise, that they understood this, that they would consider their latter end" (KJV). Do not dwell in the past. Try to focus on the court hearing and the jail time. Tomorrow will take care of itself.

Even though I know you don't need to worry yourselves about tomorrow (both of you now), I would like to suggest that you go before God and ask him to forgive you. Jim, May needs apologies from you. I will deal with that later. As of now, I would like to suggest to you, May, to forget about yourself. Jim, I would like you to do your best to seek forgiveness from those you have hurt so badly, your parents and your parents-in-law, your friends and especially your wife. If you want her to be one with you before God, she needs to forgive you. Try to humble yourself and ask for a second chance from May and others. Both you and May will be able to go to God together and ask for forgiveness. The book of prophet Isaiah says: "Come now, and let us reason together, says the LORD: Though your sins be as scarlet, they shall be as white as snow: though they be red like crimson, they shall be as wool" (Isaiah 1:18) (KJV). I hope you will try to humble yourselves before the Lord and ask for forgiveness. He is more than ready to forgive Jim. May, try to forgive him and God will listen to your prayers.

Dear May,

I enjoyed our conversation last week on the phone. Jim seemed to realize how much he has betrayed all of you – his parents, your parents, your friends, and most especially you. I hope he will stop from just talking about it and will also have a change of heart. Your mom called me a couple of days ago to tell me that Jim has been given a 6 months sentence. He is also not allowed to be around children by himself for one year after completing his time. Six months behind bars is not a joke and more so that you are expecting your baby soon. I hope you will not miss him too much.

Even though you knew that Jim would be behind bars, you thought that it would only be about three months. I can sense that it must be hard on you as well as your daughter. Will you be able to visit him before the arrival of the baby? I hope that he would like to see the baby as soon as possible when the baby arrives. Jim needs you now more than ever. He needs God to help him deal with his shame and guilt. May, love heals. I would like to suggest to you to try to forgive yourself. You tried to blame yourself for not paying enough attention to what he was doing sometimes at home, when he used to come to bed late and come home late from work. He never stopped taking his own laptop to the office. You said you had challenged him and asked why he has to take his own laptop to the office, but he had given you some excuses and you stopped asking him because you trusted him so much. We learn every day. You have learnt from your mistake. But it was not that you trusted Jim too much, it's Jim that forfeited the trust. It is okay. Try to forgive yourself and Jim as well. Your baby will arrive next month. You don't need to also carry around anger, bitterness, resentment and guilt with the baby. I don't think it's healthy for you either. You mentioned last time we spoke on the phone that you would appreciate it, if I could visit Jim in jail. This is my first week over there. He forgot that there is a consequence for any wrong behavior, but he is more than ready to change his path. I will be writing him between now and the time he will be out. Jim needs two things from you now; everyday forgiveness and amazing grace. But as I've said before, you need to forgive yourself and try to clear your mind and thought for your own sake as well as for your unborn baby. He does not need to be fed with poison – anger and bitterness are not too good for anybody, especially a pregnant woman. Try to stay healthy during the pregnancy. Forgive yourself and Jim.

I will be thinking of you. Your daughter has been asking about her dad every day. You are by yourself trying to get ready for the baby and taking care of your daughter. Continue to do a good job. I hope you will remember that you can do all things through Christ who gives you the strength you need every day (Phil. 4:13). Keep on praying and feed yourself with the words of God. Depend on him for a safe arrival of the baby and the power to continue with your daily activities. You need to be open to your in-laws help and support. All of you need support from one another. I promise to be there for you as well as Jim. God bless.

Dear May,

Congratulations on the safe arrival of your son, Jason. I am happy that both of you are doing great. You have left the hospital, and your mom and dad have come to see you. Your mom will stay with you to help out for a week and after that Jim's mom will come. You're fortunate. They will not only help you to take care of your new baby, they will also keep you company.

Jim must be happy to know that both of you and the baby are doing well. You said he was crying when you told him on the phone that your son had arrived. What do you think Jim was crying about? Maybe he is afraid that his absence at your son's birth would have a negative impact on the baby and he's probably wondering how the boy would not take after him – like father like son – that kind of fear. Are you thinking that way, too? Children are always looking for role models. I hope Jim will have a change of heart and become a new person when he gets out. Don't worry too much about that. You need to focus on taking good care of yourself and the children. Continue to pray for God's grace that you will be able to represent him not only in the children's lives but also in their dad's, too. Jim has already acknowledged his fault and he has begged you to forgive him and give him a second chance.

I have visited Jim as I promised. We had a great time together. I read John 3 with him where a noble Pharisee named Nicodemus went to Jesus and how he was told that he needed to be born again. I laid emphasis on the word born again as Jesus himself repeated it three times (John 3:3, 5, 7). Jim asked me what he needed to do. I told him that he needed to change his focus. He needed to repent of his sins and invite or re-invite Jesus Christ into his heart, since Jesus is the perfect gift of God to the world. And anyone who accepts him or believes in him will not perish but will have everlasting life. There is no judgment or condemnation for anyone who received him as his/her savior (John 3:16-18). Jim cried out and prayed for forgiveness. I believe it was a turning point in his life. We should not neglect him in jail. Try to take the baby and his sister for a visit. I believe he will be delighted to see you all.

He needs to be loved and accepted. God loves us unconditionally. We should do the same for Jim. "...While we were yet sinners, Christ died for us" (Rom 5:8) (NIV). "For all have sinned, and come short of the glory of God;" (Rom. 3:23) (KJV). I will be sending him a note to congratulate him on the safe arrival of your son. I hope you are getting enough rest and having a great time with your children. What a great opportunity to be a mom and to have parents around. Can I pray with you? Lord, we thank you for the new addition to the family, we pray that you bless him, protect him and keep him safe as well as his sister, parents and grandparents on both sides. Be with his dad, love him more and keep him safe. In Jesus name we pray.

Dear Jim,

I saw the pictures of your son. Wow! He is so handsome. What a wonderful baby. Congratulations. I am happy for both of you. When your daughter was born you were in the hospital with May, but you were not there when your son was born. How is that making you feel? I can sense that it made you feel bad! The sense of guilt and regret must be coming back to you. I can't blame you. But guess what? It was over and God represented your presence in the hospital. He was there to support May and help her to deliver the baby safely. Take it easy and let May know how sorry you are. It's not too much to ask her to forgive you again. You may also promise her that you will be a good father to your children and a good husband to her. Feel free to tell her about my visit with you and our discussions, this will authenticate what I said on your behalf that you have invited Christ into your life and that you are a new husband/father.

I was told that you asked for a weekend pass to see your baby but it was turned down. How did that make you feel? Are you thinking that the administration is thinking that maybe you wanted to go take photos of the baby so that you will be able to use it like before? Don't mind them, they do not know that it was only the old Jim who could do that but the new Jim will never think of that. If anyone is in Jesus Christ, he/she is a new person. His/her past is gone, and the new is present with him/her (II Cor. 5:17). Prove to other in-mates and guards that you are now in Christ. You don't need to say much, act it out. Actions speak louder than words. Let people in the jail know your new boss, Jesus Christ. He will never mislead you. His holy spirit will be teaching you what to do and say. Surrender yourself to the leadership of the Holy Spirit because you are now a child of God, "for all who are led by the Spirit of God are children of God" (Rom. 8:14) (NLT). You have three months plus to go. That is enough to turn the whole jail "upside down" for Christ. Let your friends know that you are no longer allowed to do what you want that may lead to trouble. You can only do what pleases God, your maker and Jesus your Lord and Saviour. Allow God to use you to bring people into his kingdom. And you know what? The government will also benefit from it. You will save the government a lot of money if some of the inmates can have "a change of heart" and never go back to jail. They, too, would go out talking to their friends about their new lives in Christ. Who knows how many lives God could change through you? Instead of feeling sorry for yourself, I would like you to see yourself as a missionary, who is there for a purpose. God can turn a horrible situation into his divine gain. The devil wanted it to be for evil, but God is making it rewarding.

If you have time before May and the children come for a visit, I would advise you to write a poem for May to express how you feel about her, how you appreciate her, and how you think she's a wonderful wife and mom. I believe you are good at that. I have read a couple of your poems. If you think you can say it when she comes, you may be too happy or sad to remember everything you would have liked to say and she too may not likely remember everything as well. So put things together on paper for her to take home. Talk to your children, too. They are young, but not too young to feel your love. Take it easy. Before you know it, you will be at home. Time goes so fast. God bless you always. Remain faithful in Christ Jesus.

Dear May,

It was great to hear that you had a wonderful time with Jim. You were not ashamed to identify yourself as his wife and the grateful mom of his two wonderful children. You were delighted with how he is making out with the Lord. He shared with you the books of Romans, Ephesians, Colossians, and first and second Corinthians. All these books in the New Testament of the Bible talk about our true identity in Christ. You said indeed, he is a new Jim. I praise God with you in that regard. Thanks for the sharing over the phone. You were not too tired to call immediately after you got home. That is great news. You know what? About two hours after our conversation, Jim also made a collect call. He was so grateful to God and to you for your visit and the children. He told me that he wrote you a nice poem and your daughter was very happy.

He has just about two months to come home. You must be excited! You both agreed to renovate your house. That will be wonderful. Can I also suggest that you need to "renovate" (renew) your marital vows! It seemed to me that you did not really know each other before your marriage. Even though there were no issues bigger than the pornography, but some other small matters were there, too. You said sometimes you were not sure how much he loved you, you were not happy about how he handled your finances. Above all, your trust for him was decreasing daily before the day of his arrest. You may have not had time to talk about such things in the jail. There is nothing wrong in writing him a letter or calling him on the phone to open the subjects. You can just make it simple; invite some of your friends to a party of renovation. Your celebration will be renovation of your house, renewal of your marriage vows and celebration of Jim's new life.

According to you, you have never been grateful to God for the lives of Jim's parents. They are prayer warriors. Since the day of Jim's arrest, his mom has never stopped fasting and praying day and night. What a remarkable woman. Yes, you are right, she is a role model to moms, especially Christian moms. They should never give up or give in for the devil. The devil should not be the lord of any children of Christians. Even though God has no grandchildren, Christians' children are children of God, too, but their parents must soak them in the blood of Jesus daily. When the devil sees the blood of Jesus on the children of Christian, he mustn't go near them, just like the plague of death passed over the Israelites in Egypt (Ex. 12:13). The devil must not touch God's anointed ones. Try to carry out what you have seen and learnt from Jim's mom. Your parents support and prayer are commendable, too. I am not surprised that God had seen you through your pregnancy. The unseen hands of God – through prayers of the faithful ones – uplifted you all the time. Greetings to all of them and tell them to keep up the good fight for Christ. You said you have started praying hard every day for your family. That is what a good wife/mom is supposed to do. It takes a good Christian mom's efforts to build a good home. Your house is now built on the rock. Continue to take good care of it.

Let me know how things are going with you. I will join you not only in counting down the days to when Jim will come home for good, but also to pray for a good reunion and a Christ centered home this time around. Keep hope alive. God bless you.

Dear Jim & May,

Welcome home, Jim. That was a great welcome home arrangement, May. It was well planned. All your siblings on both sides as well as your parents came to your house to meet Jim, while his brother went to pick him up from jail. It was a wonderful reunion.

I saw the pictures of your renovated house and the old one, too. What a big difference. Thank you for sharing the story with me. I did not know that it would turn out big and successful. Seventy-five guests including your relatives and parents from both sides were there. You were able to tell stories about how and why you renovated your house – to have a new life and new house in the same old house. You renewed your vows in the presence of all who came. Your pastor did a good job. Jim was able to testify on how he had the "born again" experience and apologized to people and asked for a second chance. All the people who came, according to what you said, enjoyed themselves and have new insight about what it meant to be a new creature in Christ. I liked how Jim laid emphasis on his new identity in Christ. He challenged people to do the same, if they have not done so before. To identify with Christ, is to be a citizen or a new citizen of the kingdom of God, that is, to become a child of God through Christ. The DVD you sent me was so clear. I love it. Thanks. Do you mind, if I share it with other people?

You have demonstrated to the people that you are a new couple. You are living in a newly renovated house with new marital vows. What you do in the public is as important as what you do in private. You have to remember that trust is not automatic- you have to earn it. You have to show each other that you are falling in love each day. Thank God that your love for each other did not dwindle during the hard time. Now you have to prove it to each other and to the public that your unconditional love for each other is growing daily in Jesus.

With regard to finances, you need to try and discipline yourselves, talk and agree on what to buy and how much to spend. Love and communication will help you to keep your marital vows and commitment intact. Effective communication and total forgiveness are highly essential in your relationship. In the house where Christ lives, joy, peace, hope, harmony, forgiveness, love and commitment and so on are supposed to be visible. Let Christ be the unseen guest in your home and silent listener to every conversation daily. You ought to communicate with God together and allow him to do so with you. You communicate with God through prayers, while he does so with you through his word (Bible). Study the Bible together. Let its principle rule your home. You must remember all the time that your identify is in Christ Jesus. You have to allow your light to shine before your children, friends, co-workers, and the people in your community.

I know that Jim is not allowed to be with children under 16 years old by himself until after one year. Through your help, May, Jim will be able to gain his community's trust back. Since God has forgiven you and you have forgiven each other and of course, Jim has also been forgiven by your four parents, I hope, Jim will be able to forgive himself totally. It is very important to do that, Jim. It is nice to know you and to come into your lives. Thanks for your trust, I will be praying for you, please do the same for me. God bless you.

Conclusion

All the seventeen chapters of the book are about 17 couples with different stories. Each of the stories, in my opinion, is applicable to many marriages, although these are not the only issues in troubled marriages. If your issues are not in this book, you can apply any story that is similar to your case. In the book, the principal solution to any troubled marriage is God. If God can be in the center of any marriage, life will be different, struggle will be easier to manage, God knows how to calm raging storm, as he did in the old days in the Bible. It is very important to remember Jesus and put one's spouse in His position. It is easy to resolve any misunderstanding when the living word is applied. For example, if there is a slip of tongue and something wanted done is omitted, it can have an adverse effect on the emotion of the spouse being offended. If care is not taken, the devil can capitalize on it, and set the couple against each other.

It is very important for each spouse to know the tactics of the enemy, the devil, he can use any means to achieve his goal. That is why it is good to categorize every situation into two; good and bad. If anything done by one's spouse annoys him/her, that is when to be cautious and chose the response wisely. God is not going to base his judgment on what the other does, but on how the one being wronged responses. Despite all Moses efforts to pray and fast for forty days and forty nights twice, his disobedience to God cost him entrance into the promise land. It was recorded in the book of Jude that demons were fighting over his body with the angels that he should go to hell. That is why Jesus said that not everyone who calls him Lord will enter the kingdom of God, but those who do the will of his father who is in heaven.

To live victoriously, for any serious Christian couple, is to surrender to the will of God, and apply his word in their relationship. Jesus' teaching in Matthew chapters 5, 6 & 7 and the writings of the Apostles on how to live as Christians, including the book of proverbs should be put into practice always. The devil should not be allowed to control your relationship, resist him and he will leave you. Treat your spouse as you would if Christ is your wife/husband.

Your marital baggage is not heavier than what God can carry, if you can give it to him. God always gives a lifetime warranty to any Christian marriage, as soon as the couple says, "I do." This warranty is supposed to be signed with the blood of Jesus Christ. All the couple needs to do is give him the driver seat of their marriage/ home and continue to be in Christ and let him be in them. Nevertheless, there is no guarantee that a Christian couple cannot have marital problems. But they need to allow Christ to be their counselor. He is the prince of peace. Any home where Christ lives, peace must be there. I am calling on the readers to invite or re-invite Christ to their homes. He is able to right the wrong.

References

Comparative Annual Divorce Rate in Canada. (n.d.). Retrieved Noyember 27, 2014, from http://www.divorcepad.com/rate/divorce-rates-in-canada.html

Countries Compared by People > Divorce rate. International Statistics at NationMaster.com. (n.d.). Retrieved November 27, 2014, from http://www. nationmaster.com/country-info/stats/People/Divorce-rate

Divorces, by province and territory. (2008). Retrieved from http://www.statcan. gc.ca/tables-tableaux/sum-som/l01/cst01/famil02-eng.htm

Government of Canada, S. D. C. S. M. and R. (2006). Family Life - Divorce / Indicators of Well-being in Canada. Retrieved from http://www4.hrsdc. gc.ca/.3ndic.1t.4r@-eng.jsp?iid=76